M60
VS
T-62

Cold War Combatants 1956–92

DAVID ISBY & LON NORDEEN

First published in Great Britain in 2010 by Osprey Publishing,
Midland House, West Way, Botley, Oxford, OX2 0PH, UK
44–02 23rd St, Suite 219, Long Island City, NY 11101, USA
E-mail: info@ospreypublishing.com

A CIP catalog record for this book is available from the British Library

Print ISBN: 978 1 84603 694 1
PDF e-book ISBN: 978 1 84908 296 9

Page layout by: Ken Vail Graphic Design, Cambridge, UK
Index by Peter Finn
Typeset in ITC Conduit and Adobe Garamond
Maps by Bounford.com
Originated by PDQ Digital Media Solutions, Suffolk, UK
Printed in China through Bookbuilders

10 11 12 13 14   10 9 8 7 6 5 4 3 2 1

Osprey Publishing is supporting the Woodland Trust, the UK's leading woodland
conservation charity, by funding the dedication of trees.

FOR A CATALOG OF ALL BOOKS PUBLISHED BY OSPREY
PUBLISHING PLEASE CONTACT:

NORTH AMERICA
Osprey Direct, c/o Random House Distribution Center, 400 Hahn Road,
Westminster, MD 21157
E-mail: uscustomerservice@ospreypublishing.com

ALL OTHER REGIONS
Osprey Direct, The Book Service Ltd, Distribution Centre, Colchester
Road, Frating Green, Colchester, Essex, CO7 7DW
E-mail: customerservice@ospreypublishing.com

www.ospreypublishing.com

Acknowledgments

The authors would like to thank: Avraham "Bren" Adan, Avi
Barber, Joseph Bermudez, Robert Butler, John Sherman Crow,
Simon Dunstan, Kenneth W. Estes, Ehud Gross, Yehuda Geller,
the IDF Armored Corps Museum – Latrun, Michael Mass, Benny
Michelsohn, Rigo Perez, Tuvya Raviv, Emanuel Sekal, Stephen
"Cookie" Sewell, Ruth Sheleh, Randy Talbot, and Steven Zaloga.

Dedication

For Steve Zaloga, *il miglior fabbro*.

Editor's note

In accordance with post-war NATO/Warsaw Pact systems of
measurement, most of the measurements given in this book are in
metric (with the exception of horsepower). For ease of comparison
between types of measurement, readers should refer to the
following conversion chart:

1 mile = 1.6km
1lb = 0.45kg
1yd = 0.9m
1ft = 0.3m
1in = 2.54cm/25.4mm
1gal = 4.5 liters
1 ton (US) = 0.9 tonnes

CONTENTS

INTRODUCTION

The US M60 and the Soviet T-62 main battle tanks (MBTs) were key to the theater military balance that, backed by nuclear deterrence, kept the Cold War cold until the revolutions of 1989 and the end of the Soviet Union in 1991. The M60 series and T-62 were evolutionary developments of the US M48 and Soviet T-54/55 tanks that made up much of the American/NATO and Soviet/Warsaw Pact armor inventory from the 1960s to the 1980s. The newer tanks added higher performance main cannon, enhanced armor, and other improvements to already proven designs. Eventual replacements for the M60 and the T-62 were the US M1 Abrams and, for the Soviets, the T-64, T-72, and eventually the T-80. These vehicles displaced, but never entirely replaced, their predecessors during the Cold War.

The roles of the M60 and the T-62 in the theater balance grew in importance in the years after they first met in combat in the 1973 Arab–Israeli (Yom Kippur) War. Both sides – especially the United States – continued to emphasize upgrading these tanks, which were poised for action in Europe. Thankfully, the two tanks never clashed in this context. Other combats, however, took place in the 1979–88 Iran–Iraq War (when Iran made extensive use of M60s and Iraq procured T-62s) and in the 1982 Lebanon War (Israeli M60A1s protected with Blazer reactive armor fought with Syrian T-62s). In the 1991 Gulf War, US Marine Corps (USMC) M60A1s penetrated Iraq's defenses on the Kuwaiti–Iraqi border and then defeated Iraqi tanks, including T-62s, to liberate Kuwait.

In the 1950s, the US Army, through the Tank and Automotive Command and other organizations, examined a number of new tank concepts to replace the earlier M46/47/48 series of Patton tanks, including the smaller lightweight high-technology T95 prototype. Yet in 1956 the US Army elected to move forward with an evolutionary upgrade to the M48, resulting in the M60. The M60 introduced improvements to all three major elements of tank design: firepower (105mm cannon), mobility (750hp diesel with more power and fuel efficiency, providing greater range), and protection (thicker armor on the cast hull and new low-profile turret). The M60 series also served with Austria, Egypt, Iran, Italy, Israel, Jordan, Oman, Saudi Arabia, Tunisia, Turkey, and Yemen. A total of 2,205 M60s, 7,653 M60A1s, 526 M60A2s, and more than 5,000 M60A3s were produced. More than half were upgrades from older M60 variants.

The T-62's 115mm smoothbore tank cannon was the primary change from the earlier T-54/55 tank designs. T-62s formed the high end of the Soviet high/low tank force mix alongside the T-54/55 from the 1960s to the 1980s. T-62s were produced in large numbers (over 19,000 in total) both to equip Soviet forces and for export, and they served with Soviet, Afghan, Algerian, Bulgarian, Cuban, Ethiopian, Egyptian, Iraqi, Iranian, Israeli, Libyan, Mongolian, Syrian, Vietnamese, and Yemeni forces. After the Cold War, they have been in service with Russia and Soviet successor states (including Belarus, Georgia, Moldova, Ukraine, and others) and there has been a thriving secondary market in exports, going to Congo and other conflict sites.

The histories of the M60 and T-62 have been shaped by a number of duels. Three of these were critical. The first "duel" was technological – the competition between US and Soviet tank development from the 1950s to the 1990s, and the similarly interactive changes in the two military warfighting organizations. The second duel was the first combat between Israeli M60s and Egyptian T-62s on the Sinai front of the 1973 Arab–Israeli War, at the battle of the Chinese Farm. Lessons from this conflict shaped the future of the M60 and the US Army, as well as the two armies that clashed. The third and final duel was the combat between US Marine Corps M60A1s and Iraqi T-62s in the 1991 Gulf War, in which US forces, who had learnt from the lessons of 1973, overwhelmed their opponents. These engagements are not the only ones in these two tanks' histories. Yet they reveal the unique nature of Cold War tank competition – the parallel development of tanks by the superpowers with combat between them occurring in proxy wars or peripheral combat against local forces.

CHRONOLOGY

1945
USA – M26 medium tank with 90mm cannon fielded in Europe;
USSR – Obiekt (Article) 137 (modified T-44 hull with new turret with 100mm cannon in place of existing 85mm) tested

1946
USSR – Obiekt 137 accepted for service as T-54

1947
USSR – Initial version of T-54 enters production

1948
USA – M46 (converted M26) with more powerful engine and new transmission enters production

1950
Korean War begins – US and NATO rearmament becomes priority
USA – M47 results from the combination of the M46 hull and T42 turret; limited use by United States, but many supplied to NATO allies. M48 featuring new turret, fire-control system, hull, and 90mm cannon enters development

Captured by the USMC Reserve 8th Tank Battalion was T-62 serial number 21121, tactical number 11A, from the 3rd Regiment, 6th Armored Brigade, 3rd Armored Division of the Iraqi Army. (Stephen Sewell)

1951
USSR – T-54 enters production with improved suspension, track, transmission, and hemispherical turret

1952
USA – M47 enters production

1953
USA – M48 enters production

1954
USSR – T-54A with fume extractor (based on captured US M26/46), gun stabilization, and infrared system enters production

1955
USSR – Obiekt 155: modified T-54 designed with nuclear, biological, chemical (NBC) defense system

1956
USA – M48A2 fitted with machine gun, fuel injection, and new suspension; US Army gains increased awareness of T-54's capabilities

1958
USSR – Obiekt 155 accepted for service and enters production as T-55, with fire-control computer and improved turret

1959
USA – M60, with 105mm cannon and diesel engine, enters production
USSR – Council of Ministers approval for Obiekt 166 program

1960
USA – M60 enters service in Europe

1961
USSR – increased awareness of M60's capabilities; Obiekt 166 accepted for service as T-62

1962

USA – M60A1, with improved turret and machine-gun cupola, enters production
USSR – T-62, with 115mm smoothbore cannon and larger hull, enters production

1967

USA – M60A2 designed with 152mm combined cannon and Shillelagh missile launcher; enters production in 1973. After many failures, most converted to Armored Vehicle Launched Bridges (AVLBs)
USSR – T-62 Model 1967 enters production

1970–71

USA – Advanced US–German MBT-70 tank program cancelled; Germans go on to produce Leopard 2

1972

USSR – T-62 Model 1972 enters production, mounting external heavy machine gun

1973

USSR – T-62 replaced in production by T-72

1976

USA – New edition of Field Manual FM100-5 *Operations*, centered on "active defense" concepts

1977

USA – M60A1 RISE Passive (RISE = Reliability Improvement of Selected Equipment)

1978

USA – M60A3 with gun stabilization, improved engine and air cleaner, computer, laser rangefinder, and tank thermal sight (TTS) sight reflects lessons of 1973 Arab–Israeli War; enters production

1981

USSR – T-62M upgrade program authorized

1982

USA – New edition of Field Manual FM100-5 *Operations* describes AirLand Battle and deep-strike concepts, making use of emerging technologies that were eventually used in 1991 Gulf War

1990

Conventional Forces in Europe (CFE) treaty signed after lengthy negotiations; limits numbers of tanks in Europe, leading to "cascade" transfers and tank scrappings

1991

USSR dissolved; Cold War ends.

"Highway to Hell" – an M60-series AVLB is positioned ready before it would be used to help bridge Iraqi antitank ditches and obstacles at the opening of the ground war. (DoD)

DESIGN AND DEVELOPMENT

Cold War tank development was a duel in itself. It differed from actual combat in that on the battlefield the "feedback loop" is immediate and decisive – the loser gets destroyed by a lethal projectile. In tank design, however, feedback comes over years rather than minutes and seconds. To lose the battle of tank development means that the opposition has a potentially better solution to tactical problems. Furthermore, a design may not fit the whole range of internal constraints: it may no longer be the best use of technology, use too many resources to build or maintain, or no longer fit how the forces that use them see the future of conflict. The evolutionary aspects of tank designs are easy to overestimate. Looking at the produced designs leading to the M60 and T-62 shows two competing linear progressions: M26–M46–M47–M48–M60 for the US and T-54–T-55–T-62 for the Soviets. These series do not, however, reflect the many discontinuities between designs, or when a successor incorporated different influences.

M60 MAIN BATTLE TANK

When US M60 tanks saw extensive action in the 1991 Gulf War against Iraq, both the tanks and the services that used them had evolved together, and were vastly different from when the M60 was designed. At the end of World War II, US Army M26 Pershing medium tanks, armed with the M3 90mm cannon, were committed to combat alongside the more numerous M4 Shermans. The M26 was the same size and weight class as the German Panzer V Panther. Both tanks had good armor protection and firepower. The 90mm cannon of the American tank fired shells with less armor penetration but greater high-explosive (HE) power than those from the Panther's long-barrel 75mm cannon. Both tanks, however, were underpowered and lacked battlefield mobility.

The first US evolutionary step beyond the M26 was the M46 Patton, developed in early 1948 and entering production in 1949. It was a converted M26 with the Continental AV-1790 air-cooled gasoline engine and CD-850 cross-drive transmission, plus other enhancements. But the most important investment was not in upgraded tanks, but in new technologies: tracks, engines, transmissions, and other configurations for future tanks. These technologies were to be incorporated in the T42, a new medium tank, lighter and faster than the M46.

While the T42 was still in prototype stage, the outbreak of the Korean War in 1950 brought new priorities: providing new tanks for combat and rearming the US Army's forces in Europe and the North Atlantic Treaty Organization (NATO) allies. What was needed was an existing design that could be put into production quickly. As the T42 was not ready in 1950, the Army mated its slim-profile turret, armed with the upgraded M36 90mm cannon, with the M46 chassis, creating the M47. An interim solution pending an improved tank, the M47 only served briefly with the US Army and Marines; 8,000 M47s were produced, most transferred to NATO members or to Austria, Iran, Jordan, South Korea, Pakistan, and other nations.

The US Army contracted with the Chrysler Corporation in late 1950 to design and develop the next tank in the Patton line, the T48 (later M48). Introducing significant improvements in design, the M48 reduced the crew to four, eliminated the hull machine gun, and incorporated improved protection – cast armor molded into an elliptical turret and a curved glacis hull. A new torsion bar suspension improved mobility. The M48 suffered from a short operating range due to its gasoline engine and small fuel tanks. Armed with the improved M41 90mm cannon, the M48 included a more advanced sighting system and rangefinder for accurate firing of chemical energy high-explosive antitank (HEAT) ammunition, which the US Army favored at the time for antitank engagements. (90mm HEAT could effectively deal with the T54/55's thick turret and glacis armor.) Rushed into production and entering US Army service in 1953, initial M48 versions suffered from many defects.

The M48 series was upgraded as production continued. The M48A1 incorporated the M1 cupola on top of the turret armed with a 12.7mm (.50-cal.) machine gun to provide protection for the tank commander, replacing the previous exposed machine-gun mounting. The M48A2 added an improved fuel-injected engine and transmission, plus an enhanced fire-control system that included the M17 coincidence rangefinder and M13A13 ballistic computer. In 1954 an improved version of the Continental Motors AVDS-1790 engine was developed, modified to use diesel and JP-4 jet fuel, and by 1957 field testing had proved this to be a reliable, fuel-efficient engine. As a result, starting in the late 1950s older M48s were modified to M48A3 configuration, which included the AVDS-1790 and additional fuel tanks (which added considerable operational range) and the improved fire-control capability introduced in the M48A2.

M60A1

This is an Israeli M60A1 of the "Serpent" battalion, which was attached to Colonel "Dani" Matt's airborne brigade that penetrated into Africa during the 1973 war. The unit received its designation in combat, as the Israeli paratroop unit insignia includes a winged serpent. This tank is identified by its serial number – 817325-Aleph – in white on a black rectangle on the hull front, with a stylized tank silhouette above it. The vehicle is basically a stock M60A1. It is distinguished by tactical markings consisting of two white rings painted around the main gun barrel (in this case), a forward-pointing white chevron marking on the rear of the turret side, aft of the spare track links (in this case), and a battalion insignia. While this tank displays a stylized serpent, other battalions had a numeral within the brigade number (numerals 1 through 4 in a shield stenciled on the left of the bumper). This battalion marking, however, was often not applied. The gun barrel markings indicate the battalion's number within the brigade. Tanks are numbered with the platoon number within the company, with the two non-command tanks having a Hebrew letter added.

Specifications
Note: M60A3 figures in square brackets if different.

Crew: 4 (commander, gunner, loader, driver)
Combat weight: 52.6 tonnes (without Blazer armor, which weighed c. 2 tonnes)
Power-to-weight ratio: 14.2hp/tonne
Engine: 750hp AVDS-1790-2A [2C] 12-cyclinder diesel
Transmission: Cross-drive, single-stage
Fuel capacity: 1,420 liters
Maximum speed (road): 48.28km/h
Range: 500km [450–80km]
Fuel consumption: 3.1 liters per km
Ground pressure: 0.87kg/cm²

Armament
Main gun: 105mm
Coaxial machine gun: 7.62mm M240
Commander's machine gun: 12.7mm M85
Main gun ammunition: 63 rounds

Protection
Hull armor: 230mm basis front; 53–48mm basis side
Turret armor: 254mm basis front; 140mm basis side; 25mm basis top; 60mm basis rear

9.3m

While the M47 saw little service with the US military, it was used extensively worldwide, including in combat during the Iran–Iraq War and other conflicts. This M47 in Somalia is being inspected by US explosive ordnance removal teams in 1992. (US DoD photo by PHCM Terry Mitchell)

The lessons of conflicts in Korea, India–Pakistan and the Middle East, and awareness of Soviet tank designs, shaped the next generation of US tanks. The examination of a Soviet Army T-54A tank by the UK military attaché in Budapest during the 1956 Hungarian rising created a shock. It was 10 tonnes lighter than the then-new M48, but was better armored (both had a 100mm glacis, but the T-54's was better sloped) and more powerfully armed (100mm vs. 90mm gun). While the M47 and M48 were being hastily pushed into production and then upgraded to keep them operationally viable, the US Army had been developing improved tank

3.2m

3.6m

technologies, including 76mm, 90mm, 105mm, and 120mm tank guns, as well as concepts such as autoloaders and low-profile and oscillating turrets. The T95 tank prototype became, in 1954, the center of US Army future tank development; the vehicle featured a low chassis with a flat track suspension similar to the T-54. The T95 program included the T53 Optical Tracking, Acquisition, and Ranging (OPTAR) system (precursor of the laser rangefinder) and compound steel with silica core armor that provided greater resistance to HEAT rounds than steel (similar in concept to the later Chobham composite armor). T95 prototypes were also used to test multiple turrets, various hydro-pneumatic suspension systems, a cross-drive transmission, and even a gas turbine engine. A total of 11 T95 prototypes were developed and tested.

In 1957, following a Congressional investigation that asked for an amphibious vehicle like the Soviet PT-76, the Joint Development Committee on Ordnance called on the Army to form a panel to review the status of Army tank design. As a result, the Army Chief of Staff, General Maxwell Taylor, organized a group to review the tank requirements for the post-1965 time period: the Ad Hoc Group on Armament for Future Tanks or Similar Combat Vehicles (ARCOVE). The initial ARCOVE report called for the testing and fielding of guided missiles as tank armament. In addition, the study called for the creation of improved types of chemical-energy warhead, target detection system, armor, and personnel protection. Taylor released a revised tank development plan, which included a recommendation to turn the light, medium, and heavy tank fleet into two types: an amphibious light tank (a reaction to Congressional encouragement) and a medium tank (eventually known as the MBT), which would perform the roles of both the medium and heavy tanks of the 1950s.

While the T95 could have led to a revolutionary US MBT, the cost of this program and development challenges led to an Army plan that recommended continued production of the M48A2 medium tank with upgrades until fiscal year (FY) 1961, when it would be supplanted by the T95 equipped with a hypervelocity cannon and new multi-fuel compression ignition engine. The AVDS-1790 diesel engine would be available for M48A2 production by late 1959 after successful prototype testing was conducted at Yuma Proving Ground in 1957. The availability of the new engine, and other development issues, led the Army to consider three options: an interim diesel-powered M48 design with a more powerful cannon and improved armor; speed up the development of the T95; or wait for a future MBT armed with a guided missile system and radiological protection (recommended by the ARCOVE study). The decision was made to cancel the T95, keep the future tank in research and development (which led to the missile-armed M60A2 and ambitious US/German MBT-70 programs), and procure the M60 as an interim tank.

In June 1958, the XM60 interim tank program combined the M48A2 chassis, the AVDS-1790, modifications to the hull and turret to incorporate siliceous core armor (pending the outcome of further tests), and a new cannon to be decided after a comparative test firing trial held at Aberdeen Proving Ground in October 1958. In these trials, the British-developed 105mm X15E8 used armor-piercing discarding sabot (APDS) antitank ammunition to outperform the Ordnance Department's preferred option, the T123E6 120mm cannon, as well as a 90mm smoothbore cannon firing armor-piercing fin-stabilized discarding sabot (APFSDS) projectiles and the existing 90mm cannon with improved T300 HEAT rounds.

The XM60 was to have frontal protection to survive hits from the T-54/55's 100mm cannon with an armor-piercing capped (APC) round at a range of approximately 1,500m. Siliceous core armor caused the redesign of the M60 hull into a flat, square shape and led to modifications to the turret. Yet when this armor proved to be costly and hard to manufacture, it was dropped from the M60 program. The forward hull of the M60 was a single piece of cast steel 120mm thick at an angle of 64 degrees for an equivalent of about 230mm of rolled homogenous armor (RHA) protection. The M60 turret was a single casting similar to the M48.

Rushed into production in 1959, after 360 M60 tanks were built at the Chrysler Newark, Delaware plant, production then switched to the Detroit Tank Arsenal, where the bulk of the 2,205 M60s were made. The M60 was deployed first to US Army tank units in the US in 1959 and then with the 3rd Armored Division in Germany.

There were three compartments in the M60: driver's in the front, fighting compartment in the middle, and engine/transmission at the rear. The driver sat in the middle with ammunition racks on either side, and was provided with three M27 periscopes and an M24 infrared periscope for night operations. There was a single-piece hatch cover overhead. The center-mounted M60 turret was driven by a Cadillac Gage hydraulic system, which provided both turret rotation and gun correction. The loader was located on the left and commander and gunner on the right of the turret. Located at the rear of the turret, the tank commander had a large cupola overhead, which was fitted with all-around vision blocks and an M28 (upgraded to the M36 or M36 in the M60A1) sight, plus an M85 12.7mm machine gun. Cupola rotation was done by a hand crank and a hatch provided on the top, which rotated to the rear for entrance and exit. The gunner was in front of and seated lower than the tank commander. He utilized an M31 (upgraded to M32 in the M60A1) periscope and battlesight with 8x power magnification or M32 clear/infrared periscope for day and night operations, and an M105C (M105D in the M60A1) telescope for fire-control of the 105mm cannon. At the rear of the tank was the engine compartment containing the Continental AVDS-1792-2A 12-cylinder, air-cooled diesel engine, General Motors cross-drive transmission, and fuel tanks. An armored bulkhead separated the engine compartment from the crew.

In early 1960, Chrysler was awarded a contract to design an improved turret. By mid 1961, three pilot production vehicles were available for a test program. The M60E1 (later redesignated M60A1) featured a new turret with an elongated nose that provided improved ballistic protection (equal to the flat glacis of the hull), greater room for the crew, and additional ammunition storage (total 63 rounds vs. 60 for the M60) at the rear bustle. The improved M60A1 turret had a more angled shape (providing smaller frontal surface area and more stowage in the rear) with a larger gun opening for the 105mm cannon, wider diameter commander's cupola, plus thicker armor of 250mm at the turret front (140mm sides). The M60A1 was, like the M60, armed with the UK-designed M68 rifled 105mm cannon and carried 63 rounds of 105mm ammunition: 26 rounds in racks located on either side of the driver in the forward hull, 13 in ready-to-use racks in the turret, and the remainder in the turret bustle. In addition, there were 5,000 rounds for the 7.62mm coaxial machine gun and 500 rounds for the 12.7mm machine gun, plus hand grenades, M3 submachine guns, and ammunition for crew self-defense. In October 1962, the M60A1 went into production at the Detroit Arsenal.

T-62

This is an Egyptian T-62 Model 1967 of the 25th Armored Brigade in the 1973 Arab–Israeli War. It is basically a stock T-62. It is marked in two-tone camouflage, although most Egyptian tanks had single-tone camouflage and used Arabic numerals for tactical markings.

Specifications

Crew: 4 (commander, gunner, loader, driver)
Combat weight: 40 tonnes
Power-to-weight ratio: 19.17hp/tonne
Engine: 580hp V-55V V-12 diesel
Transmission: Mechanical synchromesh
Fuel capacity: 675 liters internal + 285 liters external
Maximum speed (road): 50km/h
Range: 450km
Fuel consumption: 1.9–2.1 liters/km
Ground pressure: 0.83kg/cm^2

Armament
Main gun: 115mm U-5TS
Co-axial machine gun: 7.62mm PKT
Commander's machine gun: 12.7mm DShkM (not on this model)
Main gun ammunition: 40

Protection
Hull armor: 100mm @ 60° (200mm basis) front; 80mm @ 0° (80mm basis) side
Turret armor: 170mm rounded (200mm basis) front; 120mm basis side; 30mm basis top; 40mm rounded (60mm basis) rear

9.3m

While the US Army of the 1950s and 1960s relied primarily on HEAT for its 90mm tank guns, the M60A1 in 1973 usually carried a mix of M393 APDS-Tracer (APDS-T) antitank rounds (weight 18.6kg; 1,458m/sec muzzle velocity; more than 250mm maximum armor penetration); M393 high-explosive squash head (HESH, also known in the United States as HEP – high-explosive, plastic) rounds for use against fortifications and tanks; M456 HEAT rounds (penetrating 430mm of armor at any range), and M416 smoke rounds. The APDS projectile, after leaving the gun tube, dropped its sabot, which filled the full size of the bore and ensured effective

A classic T-62 Model 1967, without the 12.7mm DShKM heavy machine gun that distinguished the Model 1972 and subsequent production. Unlike T-55s, few early production T-62s were retrofitted with the machine gun. (US DoD)

2.4m

3.3m

propulsion. This left the small, heavy fast-spinning penetrator (dense tungsten carbide steel with low aerodynamic drag) to hit the target. On impact it penetrated armor purely due to its kinetic energy. There were cases, however, where shells glanced off due to the extreme angle of the glacis and rounded turrets of the Soviet tanks. The HEAT rounds could penetrate the armor of any Soviet-built tank, but the velocity of this projectile was slower than that of an APDS round and the projectile-to-armor impact angle had to be such that the nose-mounted fuze could operate to detonate the HEAT warhead. The HEAT round was also susceptible to cross-winds, since it was fin stabilized.

T-62 (OBIETK 166) MAIN BATTLE TANK

The pre-1973 war exports of T-62s to Egypt and Syria were followed by sales to many other Arab armies and other markets, but not the Warsaw Pact allies (who never set up their own production lines, unlike with the T-55). This is an Algerian Army T-62 Model 1967 at a parade in the 1980s. (US DoD)

At the end of World War II, and in reaction to the German Tiger and Panther threats, the Soviet Army was fielding improved T-44 medium and IS-3 heavy tanks. Based on wartime experience, the Soviets focused on the tank as their primary battlefield weapon and new versions were expected every few years. The T-54 medium tank, with a powerful 100mm cannon and excellent armor, was introduced in 1946 and the improved T-55 in 1958.

In the mid 1950s, advances in Western armor such as the M48, XM60, and the British Chieftain prompted the Soviets to upgrade their frontline tanks. Two paths

were followed. The Obietk 165 design was an improved T-55 with a more capable long-barrel (62-caliber) 100mm cannon. Obietk 166 was a longer tank, intended originally as a long-range tank destroyer rather than an MBT. It was armed with a new smoothbore 115mm cannon developed under the codename Rapira 3, firing a high-velocity APFSDS round that had a flat trajectory out to 1,500m and less of a requirement for a precision rangefinder.

The T-62 design did not take a direct, linear progression. Like the M60, the T-62 was designed in response to the capabilities of the opposing superpower's tanks. Also like the M60 design, it was intended as an interim measure. The future would belong to the high-technology Obietk 430 (which, as the T-64A, did not enter production until 1969 instead of 1962 as planned) or a number of projects with a missile as their main armament (and which, like the US M60A2, never worked out in practice). Obietk 166, redesignated T-62 after adoption, had greater firepower, weapons load, and mobility than heavy tanks such as the 122mm-armed T-10M or assault guns such as the ISU-122.

The adoption of smoothbore cannon technology was a response to the M48's cast armor hull. Similarly, the increase of the T-62's main gun to the 115mm U-5TS Molot (hammer) was a response to the NATO 105mm tank gun, and the T-64's 125mm smoothbore was designed to maintain a caliber advantage over the British Chieftain's 120mm gun. The T-62 had the most advanced gun in the world at the time of its introduction, but by costing 50 percent more than the T-55, it was never built in the numbers required to replace completely the T-54/55 in the Soviet Army's armored force.

The T-62 had a 100mm glacis angled at 60 degrees, which presented about 200mm RHA armor protection. Turret armor ranged from 230mm in the front to 120mm on the sides and 60mm at the rear, and its very rounded shape added to its effectiveness. Other T-62 features included an overpressure NBC defense system, although the crew still had to wear cumbersome protective clothing and masks if they were going to use their weapons. The T-62 was designed to use a range of engineer equipment: dozer blades, mine rollers, and mine plows. While the T-62 was praised for its high firepower, mobility, and good armor, the tank was small, had terrible human engineering, was hard to drive, and had a limited ammunition load of only 40 rounds.

The T-62 was paraded for the first time in 1965. Soviet T-62s first saw action in the 1968 invasion of Czechoslovakia and in the 1969 border fighting with China (when one was knocked out and captured). By 1973, T-62s equipped more than three-quarters of the Group of Soviet Forces in Germany. Unlike the earlier T-54/55, the T-62 did not equip the Soviets' Warsaw Pact clients (the Bulgarians bought 100, then resold them), but more distant export clients would provide the opportunities for large-scale combat.

THE BATTLE OF THE CHINESE FARM, 1973

During the 1967 Six-Day War, Israel defeated Egyptian, Syrian, and Jordanian military forces and captured the Sinai Peninsula, Golan Heights, and West Bank territories. By 1973, the Arab–Israeli confrontation had become another example of a Soviet–US proxy conflict. This situation was reflected in the sources of each side's MBTs. The Arabs relied on the Soviets and the Israelis (increasingly) on the United States, even though the tanks themselves were designed for use in a future theater conflict in Europe. Yet while the combatants had to rely on outside sources for tanks, the way they trained, equipped, organized, and used them were their own.

ISRAELI FORCES

Because of their success in the Six-Day War, the Israelis had de-emphasized the use of combined arms tactics on the battlefield. Many thought that against Arab opponents a tank-heavy force would again be successful. In the years after the War of Attrition (1967–70), General David "Dado" Elazar and Major General Israel Tal (former Chief of Staff, Armored Corps), then respectively Chief and Vice Chief of Staff of the Israel Defense Forces (IDF), advocated funding primarily for the air force and secondarily for tank-dominated armored units. Infantry (even the elite paratroopers), artillery, engineers, and

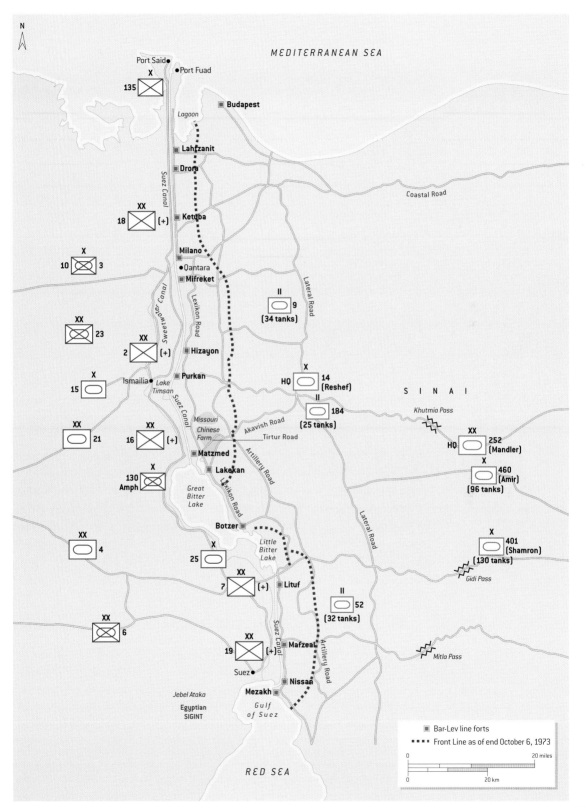

N

MEDITERRANEAN SEA

Port Said
Port Fuad

X 135

Budapest

Lagoon

Lahtzanit

Drora

Coastal Road

XX 18 (+)

Ketuba

Milano

X 10 3

Qantara

Mifreket

II 9
(34 tanks)

Lateral Road

XX 23

XX 2 (+)

Hizayon

Suez Canal

Sweetwater Canal

Lexikon Road

X 15

Ismailia

Lake Timsan

Purkan

HQ X 14
(Reshef)

S I N A I

Khutmia Pass

II 184
(25 tanks)

XX 21

XX 16 (+)

Missouri
Chinese
Farm

Akavish Road

Tirtur Road

HQ XX 252
(Mandler)

X 460
(Amir)
(96 tanks)

Matzmed

Lakekan

Artillery Road

X 130
Amph

Great
Bitter
Lake

Lexikon Road

Botzer

Little
Bitter
Lake

X 401
(Shamron)
(130 tanks)

Gidi Pass

XX 4

X 25

XX 7 (+)

Lituf

II 52
(32 tanks)

Lateral Road

XX 6

Suez Canal

XX 19 (+)

Mafzeal

Artillery Road

Mitla Pass

Suez

Nissan

Mezakh

Jebel Ataka

Egyptian
SIGINT

Gulf
of Suez

Bar-Lev line forts

Front Line as of end October 6, 1973

0   20 miles

0   20 km

RED SEA

19

the navy received what was left. Major General Avraham "Bren" Adan, Chief of the Armored Corps until the 1973 war, was just starting to field M113 armored personnel carriers (APCs) to replace the aging US-built M3 halftracks, and also to upgrade the capabilities of armored infantry – part of the Armored Corps along with self-propelled (SP) artillery – to allow the tanks to fight a fast-moving combined arms battle.

Israel on the eve of the 1973 war had 2,209 (2,138 operational) MBTs. These included:

- 709 upgraded Centurions (Sh'ot Cal, "scourge" in Hebrew) with the same 105mm gun and diesel engine as the M48/60
- 314 unmodernized Centurions
- 445 upgraded M48s (known as Magach 3s, "battering ram" in Hebrew) with 105mm cannon and diesel engines
- 150 M60A1s (known as Magach 6As)
- 146 captured T-54/55s (Tiran 4/5) upgraded with the M68 105mm cannon and Browning machine guns
- 374 Sherman M50/51s upgraded with French-designed lightweight 75mm or 105mm cannon.

The Israeli Army of 1967–73 was in essence a tank army. While the Israeli Air Force (IAF) faced the challenge of dealing with Egypt's integrated air defense system (IADS) in the War of Attrition, the IDF's Armored Corps was seen as the victors of 1967, and faced no adversary during this period of conflict from which to draw new lessons. They were an elite force, with their conscripts earning their black berets and taking their oath in torchlight ceremonies at the ancient fortress of Masada. Female conscripts competed for a limited number of non-combat maintenance and training slots that allowed them to receive tank driver training.

In the early 1970s, Israeli tank crews went through seven months of initial training divided into three phases, with different programs for those headed for the Sh'ot Cal or Magach tanks. Basic training went on for 11 weeks and focused on field training, small arms handling, and conditioning. This was followed by two months of tank crew training at the Armor Academy, where the students were divided into drivers and turret crews of gunners, loaders, and communications specialists. The tank commanders were added, forming crews. The final phase, about two months in length, included field training at the crew, platoon, and company levels in the Sinai or Negev Desert.

At the end of training, tank crews were assigned to active duty units – especially the 252nd Armored Division in the Sinai or the 7th Armored Brigade in the Golan – where they operated for about two years. After their initial service was complete, the integral crews (they stayed together throughout active and reserve service) were assigned to a reserve unit, where tankers selected for training as reserve officers would join them as platoon leaders after an additional year of training. While reserve training was often inadequate, the Israelis never slacked off on tank gunnery, which they saw as the one indispensable skill.

In the early 1970s, Sherman M50/51 battalions were assigned to mechanized units and Sh'ot Cal, Magach, and Tiran battalions assigned to armored brigades. Reserve brigades trained annually and had equipment stockpiled for mobilization close to the potential battle areas. It took about 72 hours for the IDF to mobilize reserve forces and move them to battlezones, assuming no disruptions.

Because of the Israeli reliance on reserve forces, high-readiness units were often the first to receive new equipment. Older equipment, however, was often kept in service with reserve units for many years, because that is what the crews trained on during active service and it was costly to recall them for retraining. While the basic M48A2 had entered Israeli service in the mid 1960s, sold by Germany and the United States and used in the fighting of 1967, the first of 150 new Magach 6A M60A1s were delivered to Israel from 1971. They entered service with a 36-tank battalion at the Armored School (which had an operational mission on mobilization) and then with the 600th Armored Brigade and 87th Reconnaissance Battalion, both reserve units committed to reinforce the Sinai front. Colonel Tuvya Raviv formed the 600th Armored Brigade: "I was appointed the commander of the 600th Armored Brigade in September 1971 when the brigade did not exist. I guess I got the job as a result of my considerable armor experience… I had to establish the 600th Armored Brigade from nothing and for that mission I got experienced tank veterans from the [1969–70] static war and new M60A1 tanks which were not equipped with all of the required systems, such as no machine guns etc. My brigade finished training just weeks before the 1973 war."

Yehuda Geller also served in the new brigade: "I completed my basic training in the late 1950s using the Sherman M50 and the French AMX-13 light battle tanks, and served my reserve duty from 1961 to 1973 as the commander of reconnaissance units of the reserve and regular Armored Corps… The 600th Brigade was equipped with 111 M60A1 tanks according to the IDF standard, in three battalions: 407th, 409th, and 410th. Each battalion included 36 tanks plus three at the brigade headquarters."

A T-62 of the Egyptian 25th Armored Brigade, photographed near Kabrit in Egypt in February 1974 after disengaging from positions in the Sinai. (United Nations via Steven Zaloga)

1973 – ISRAELI AND EGYPTIAN TACTICAL TANK ORGANIZATION

Israeli armor in the early 1970s was organized into three-tank platoons, 11-tank companies (three platoons, two HQ tanks) and 36-tank battalions (including three tanks at the battalion HQ). Some battalions had four companies. Egyptian armor in the 1973 war was supposed to be organized on the Soviet model (three-tank platoons, company of three platoons plus an HQ tank, battalion of three companies plus an HQ tank), but shortages of tanks led to the use of a number of modified tables of organization. Some units fielded 22-tank battalions (one platoon missing from each company) or 21-tank (or SU-100 assault gun) battalions (one company missing).

The 87th Reconnaissance Battalion, equipped with 24 new US-supplied M60A1 tanks as well as 36 M113 APCs, was formed in May 1973 as a part of the reserve 143rd Armored Division. Commanded by Lieutenant Colonel Ben-Zion "Benny" Carmeli, the 87th's personnel were high-readiness reservists that had just completed their active service; the 87th was their first reserve posting.

In the Sinai, the forward line of defense rested on the Bar-Lev Line of 22 major forts and many smaller fortifications located along the Suez Canal and built during the War of Attrition. It was not a static defense line, but was used for surveillance of Egyptian activities and to act as a deterrent. In October 1973, only 14 forts were manned, garrisoned by the 68th Infantry Battalion from the second-line reserve 16th Brigade from Jerusalem. The defense of the Sinai was the responsibility of Israeli Southern Command under Lieutenant General Shmuel Gonen. Major General Albert Mandler commanded the regular force 252nd Armored Division with 280 Magach tanks in three armored brigades: 14th Armored Brigade under Colonel Amnon Reshef, forward deployed in the center; 460th Armored Brigade under Colonel Gabi Amir, located in the north; 401st Armored Brigade led by Colonel Dan Shamron in the south. The armored units were supported by 12 batteries of artillery.

Many of the division's supporting units such as armored infantry and additional artillery were reserve forces. Not only were the forward deployed tank units lacking in mechanized infantry support, but their ammunition racks were filled primarily with APDS rounds to halt armor attacks. After mobilization, the regular forces were backed up by six armored and mechanized brigades grouped into two reserve armored divisions: 143rd "Pillar of Fire" led by Major General Ariel "Arik" Sharon and 162nd "Iron" led by Adan. All Magach tanks were committed to the Sinai; the rocky Golan terrain was considered unsuited to their US-design track pads. Of the 1,088 tanks planned for commitment to the Sinai front, 54 percent were Magach 3s and 14 percent Magach 6As.

In the event of a major Egyptian assault across the Canal, the Israeli war plan, Operation *Dovecote*, called for more than 20 batteries of mobile artillery to be in the Sinai plus two of 252nd Armored Division's armored brigades to be in position between the Canal and the Israeli-built Artillery Road (8–10km east of the Canal) supported by the third armored brigade (25km back from the Canal). But these units were not in their battle positions on October 6, 1973, when the war began. Despite

Early 1970s – a three-tank platoon of Israeli Magach 6As (M60A1s) halts during training in the Sinai. These tanks are unmodified and are still fitted with their original US T97 tracks and high Mk 19 cupola, both of which the Israelis eventually replaced. (Michael Mass – IDF Armored Corps Museum)

multiple warnings of impending hostilities, neither the national government nor Gonen wanted to be seen as provoking a confrontation, despite the threat of war. Only some three tanks and 28 artillery pieces were positioned to fire on the Egyptian crossing of the Canal (and many of these did not survive well-planned air, artillery, and special forces attacks) and only one of the three brigades was within striking range of the Canal incursion. The rest of the forces were concentrated in assembly areas back from the Canal when the war began.

EGYPTIAN FORCES

Following their 1967 defeat, Egypt and Syria rebuilt their armies and air forces. With the assistance of the Soviet Union, they worked with the Soviet General Staff to create war plans to cross the Suez Canal, achieve a foothold in the Sinai, and push Israeli forces from the Golan Heights. The goal was to use Arab strengths in material, manpower, artillery, and tanks to overcome Israeli advantages in airpower and mobility.

The Soviet Union supplied the Egyptian and Syrian armies with some 3,000 T-54/55/62 MBTs and provided intensive training. Egypt received about 200 then-new T-62s; most equipped the newly formed 15th and 25th Independent Armored Brigades, assigned to the Second and Third Armies respectively. Keeping the new tanks concentrated in these brigades, intended to be army-level reserves, eased maintenance support and prevented their increased combat power being dissipated. It also reflected political concerns – proposals to re-equip one armored division with T-62s instead were blocked by worries over the commanding general's political reliability (he was subsequently exiled as an attaché). The Egyptians, promised more T-62s, broke relations with the USSR in July 1972 after the Soviets had delayed delivery.

To operate the new tanks, the Egyptians gave the military first claim on the country's manpower. Every tank commander was to be a university, high school, or technical school graduate. Egyptian training focused on the Canal crossing; tank operations in the Sinai or even basic skills such as tank gunnery were not training priorities. Most tank gunners got to fire three or fewer main gun rounds a year.

The Egyptian use of the T-62 in 1973 was an example of their long-standing practice of diverging from great power models and organizing around key weapons. The Egyptian armored force of 1973 was not intended to duplicate the rapid conventional advance of the Soviet units they were modeled on. They were there to back up the infantry which, unlike those of 1967, were equipped and trained with large numbers of antitank weapons.

THE CONFLICT

War began on the afternoon of October 6, 1973, the Jewish holy day of Yom Kippur and also part of the Muslim holy month of Ramadan, with a simultaneous assault by both Egyptian and Syrian forces. The Egyptian Second Army was responsible for northern Sinai from Port Said to Fayid, while the Third Army had the southern sector. Additional armored divisions and mechanized brigades were positioned on the western side of the Suez Canal. This massive force included 300,000 troops equipped with 2,000 pieces of artillery and more than 1,600 tanks.

Operation *Badr* included a crossing along the full length of the Suez Canal under the cover of a massive artillery barrage (nearly 1,500 guns) and air and special forces attacks. The assault and artillery/air suppression was so successful that only 208 Egyptians were killed and 20 tanks and 15 planes lost during the crossing. A multi-divisional force of infantry, armor, artillery, and air defense units crossed into the Sinai and took up pre-planned defensive positions. Within hours, Egyptian forces had set up more than a dozen crossing points using ferries and pontoon bridges and established a defensive line 10–15km into the Sinai, protected by a strong air defense shield and infantry units armed with large numbers of antitank weapons: RPG-7 rocket launchers, Malyutka (NATO codename AT-3 *Sagger*) antitank guided missiles (ATGMs), and a full range of antitank guns. A large force was also maintained on the Egyptian side as a reserve against Israeli armored thrusts and to protect the 100 surface-to-air missile (SAM) and anti-aircraft artillery (AAA) batteries to defend against the Israeli air force.

In response, Israeli tanks from 252nd Armored Division advanced in small groups. Initial reports were that the Egyptian attack was only a raid. Some of the tanks advanced to the Canal, inflicting casualties on Egyptian forces and supporting the evacuation of Israeli troops from surrounded Bar-Lev Line forts. Most of the advancing Israeli tank columns, however, were ambushed by Egyptian infantry, special forces (one 600th Armored Brigade M60A1 battalion was hit while trying to unload from its transporter trucks), and T-54/55 tanks (the T-62s were part of the reserve). The IAF jets ran into a wall of Egyptian SAMs and anti-aircraft fire as they flew in to hit the crossing sites.

By dawn on October 7, more than 50,000 Egyptian infantry, 400 tanks, and hundreds of artillery pieces were entrenched in the Sinai. The 252nd Armored Division's tanks continued to move forward to rescue surrounded Bar-Lev defenders and counterattack. With little support from artillery or infantry (still mobilizing) or aircraft (held at bay by air defenses), the Israelis met heavy fire from ATGMs, RPGs, recoilless rifles, and tank guns. By early afternoon, Mandler reported his division was down to about 100 tanks.

Late in the afternoon of October 7, Gonen, Adan, and Mandler, joined by Chief of Staff General Elazar, met at Southern Command HQ. Elazar said the focus of most air support and command attention on October 8 would be on stopping the dangerous Syrian advance on the Golan Heights. Yet he also ordered a limited attack by the 162nd Armored Division against the Egyptian Second Army bridgehead, to advance no closer than 2–3km from the Canal. The 143rd Armored Division was to hold to the east of the battlefield at Tasa on the main road from Israel as a reserve to support any success or hold the line in the event of failure.

Israeli forces were ordered to form a defensive line between the Artillery and Lateral Roads, 10–30km east of the Canal. As forward elements of the two reserve divisions started to arrive, Gonen reorganized and redistributed forces, assigning the 162nd Armored Division to the northern sector, the 143rd Armored Division to the central sector, and the 252nd Armored Division's remaining units to the southern sector. Mandler was later killed by Egyptian artillery fire directed by signals intelligence, and was replaced by Major General Kalman Magen.

After midnight, General Gonen changed the plan. The 162nd was to attack from Qantara toward the Great Bitter Lake. If enough tanks were available, the 143rd Armored Division was to strike in the same area. Two of 162nd Armored Division's brigades, Colonel Nathan "Natke" Nir's 217th Armored Brigade and Colonel Gabi Amir's 460th Armored Brigade, advanced toward their assigned jumping off locations starting around 0400hrs. Around dawn, Nir's forces engaged in a battle in the Qantara sector with elements of the Egyptian 18th Infantry Division supported by two companies of T-62 tanks from the 15th Armored Brigade. Gonen requested that Nir's tanks stay in action, which saw Sh'ot Cal tanks battle with T-62s in two separate engagements, with both sides suffering losses.

This engagement left Amir's two armored battalions, with 50 Sh'ot Cal tanks, to attack the Egyptian 2nd Infantry Division's two entrenched brigades. While one tank battalion had to be pulled back to rearm and refuel, the other, under Lieutenant Colonel Haim Adini, attacked at around 1100hrs. It penetrated to within 800m of the Canal before 18 of its 25 tanks were knocked out. A second, larger, attack toward the Firdan bridgehead by both Amir's and Nir's brigades in early afternoon was also fought to a standstill. The 162nd Armored Division had suffered more than 80 tanks destroyed and damaged. Later in the day, Egyptian forces pushed further into the Sinai under the cover of artillery and missile fire.

Uncoordinated counterattacks by undersized tank forces and by airstrikes had failed to achieve success for the Israelis, and cost more than 250 tanks and 25 aircraft in the first three days of the fighting on the Sinai front. The Israelis formed a defensive line and brought forward reserve units. Throughout the Sinai front, depleted Israeli armored units were rebuilt and tactics modified. Armored forces were teamed with infantry mounted in halftracks or M113 APCs and SP artillery to form combined arms task forces.

The 87th Reconnaissance Battalion, mobilized on October 6, held the line in the Sinai. Its popular commander was lost to an artillery barrage on October 8, Major Yoav Brom assuming command. The 87th later was assigned to the weakened 14th Brigade, which had been sent from the 252nd Armored Division to the 143rd. On the night of October 9, units of the battalion, demonstrating their reconnaissance skills, infiltrated to the Suez Canal and discovered the weak spot between the Egyptian Second and Third Armies, which later became the site for the bridgehead across the Canal. The 87th also scouted and patrolled the southern sector assigned to the 14th Armored Brigade.

Ehud Gross was among the reinforcements who took the M60 tank into action:

At the beginning of the war on October 6, 1973, I was a young major in the education department of the IDF. I had no assigned mobilization role in a combat unit, but I had a lot of experience in tanks and commanding, starting with the battles for the water sources against the Syrians in 1965, then as a tank platoon commander in the 1967 war in battles against the Jordanians and the battles on the Golan Heights against the Syrians. At the start of the 1973 war, I called the Armor Corps headquarters looking for a free unit of tanks to participate in. First I was sent to the 421st Armored Brigade as a battalion commander, but the original deputy commander who I was supposed to replace showed up, so I was sent to the 407th Tank Battalion of the 600th Armored Brigade as a company commander. I was assigned to command A Company. I had experience on various versions of the Sherman, M48 Patton, and then the upgraded M48A3/Magach 3, so I knew armor. I was very impressed with the M60A1 which I now commanded. It was fast, stable, roomy, reliable, and quite well equipped (except for no night sights!) and had a large supply of rounds for its 105mm cannon. I had to study quickly to understand all of the capabilities of this new tank. At the start of the war, we were engaged in defensive battles with high mobility in the central zone area of the Sinai.

Yehuda Geller was another replacement for those lost in the opening tank battles:

Following my initiative, and injury to both [previous] commanders of the 410th Battalion of the 600th Brigade [Lieutenant Colonels Amnon Marton and Yehuda Bachar], I was appointed as commander of the 410th Battalion on the third day of the Yom Kippur War; and that was the first time I mounted the IDF Patton tank. My personal experience regarding the technological aspects of the M60 was very limited… During the first week of the war, the 409th and 410th Battalions were engaged in a holding action and attacks, and following the breakthrough, in exerting constant pressure toward the north against the southern flank of the Second Egyptian Army, in order to expand and ensure a communication and transportation corridor to the Canal's western side.

An Israeli M60A1 modified with an externally mounted M1919 Browning machine gun for use by the loader (or supporting infantry). The tactical marking on the fender shows the battalion insignia – usually a number within its brigade, in this case it is a stylized serpent. (Steven Zaloga)

The grave situation for Israel on the Golan Heights was stabilized on October 8. An Israeli counterattack to push back Syrian forces opened on October 11, and in response the Syrians demanded further Egyptian attacks to draw away Israeli resources. On October 14, the Egyptian armor moved forward from their defensive positions deeper into the Sinai in what became the largest tank battle since World War II. The 21st Armored Division led the Second Army and the 4th Armored Division led the Third Army attacks, with T-54/55-equipped units in front. Most of the 15th and all of the 25th Armored Brigade's T-62s were initially kept in reserve to exploit a breakthrough that never came. Some T-62s from the 15th and a few from the 25th ended up taking part in the unsuccessful Egyptian attacks.

Israeli armor, with support from artillery and aircraft, knocked out more than 250 Egyptian tanks and 200 other vehicles for the loss of fewer than 40 of their own, and then immediately shifted over to a counterattack. The 87th Reconnaissance Battalion participated in defensive actions against the Egyptian 21st Armored Division attack on October 14, and then launched a successful but costly counterattack; personnel casualties included seven dead and many wounded. Ehud Gross' company had also been part of the battle:

> In war, Israeli forces are flexible and after a few days' fighting my unit was assigned to the 14th Armored Brigade under Colonel Reshef, who had been reassigned to Major General Sharon's 143rd Division in the central Sinai. His brigade was equipped with M48A3 Magach 3 tanks. My unit was known as "Alef" after the first letter of the Hebrew alphabet, with the call sign of "Ahava," which means love. So you can imagine I would call [in clear voice, standard Israeli radio practice at that time] over the radio to my forces looking for love. Our units stopped the Egyptian attack on October 14 in the central sector and inflicted heavy losses on the Egyptian 1st Mechanized Brigade.

The following day, the Israelis began their offensive in the Sinai. This led to the intense three-day battle of the Chinese Farm, which was named after a Japanese agricultural aid project in the area, abandoned in 1967, whose irrigation canals and overgrown vegetation constituted an obstacle to tank forces. The Israeli objective of Operation *Brave Heart* was to cross the Suez Canal into Africa, outflank the Second and Third Armies, and turn the tide in the Sinai. The 87th Reconnaissance Battalion led the assault to the Canal for the 14th Armored Brigade (now reduced to 39 tanks), and achieved its initial objectives of penetrating the defenses at night.

Ehud Gross' company was one of the spearhead units:

We then went into action to clear out Egyptian forces near Great Bitter Lake to open the way for the crossing of the Suez Canal and the assault into Egyptian Territory to outflank their penetration into the Sinai. We moved forward along the Lexicon Road toward the Suez Canal and ran into heavy concentrations of Egyptian forces, which fought with intensity. At the beginning of the night battle, my mission was to clear the Akavish Road to enable the first unit (a mix of armor and paratroopers) to cross the Suez Canal and establish the bridgehead. This mission was successfully accomplished and I was waiting in the middle of the night with five tanks out of nine, because two of my tanks were hit in the clearing of Akavish Road, and I sent two other tanks to tow these to the ordnance center for repair. I heard on the radio net the results of ongoing fighting and even though we were sure to face sudden death or injury and it would be like a suicide mission, I did not want to carry the shame of being a non-initiative commander, so I urged my commander Colonel

Leaving Africa – Israeli M60A1s withdraw from their bridgehead following the 1973 war, moving first into Sinai on the east side of the Mitla and Gidi Passes and, eventually, back to Israel itself. (Steven Zaloga)

Reshef to launch my unit into the area known as "the Thopet" (hell) near the Lexicon–Tartur Junction. I passed up another slower unit and pressed on and when I got close to the junction, I gave an order to load a squash head round [HESH] into the gun because I did not know if we would face tanks or infantry or missile teams…

A too-common sight in October 1973: this M60A1 suffered a catastrophic kill, probably the result of the hydraulic fluid lines near the turret race "cooking off" and detonating ammunition. (Michael Mass – IDF Armored Corps Museum)

The very second I gave the order, I felt a great shock followed by darkness. First I thought we were hit by a missile, but only much later did I find out we were hit by a 100mm shell from a T-55 fired at a range of only 40m. We had five crew in the tank, as I had given my tank to the deputy brigade commander. The loader touched my leg and yelled "Yossi is dead!" Yossi was the tank platoon commander I controlled at that hour. The tank was not moving and started to smoke and burn. I ordered the crew to bail out but to not forget the maps and PRC [communications] device. A short while later the tank exploded and the turret flew up into the air and rotated 180 degrees, turned over, and landed on its ring. Soon enough I realized I was injured by fragments and was bleeding, but I had to go on. I was the senior officer on the ground, surrounded by more than 20 burned and damaged tanks and 20–30 survivors; I had to lead the injured tankers and armored infantry survivors back to our forces in the south. While aiding the force, mortars landed among us causing further injuries, including to our only trained aid-man, who we now put on a stretcher and carried. It was extremely foggy and we heard tank engines. Suddenly I saw tank cannon and I ran forward and waved my arms and prayed… Yelling "Don't shoot!" I went up and met my colleague, the third company commander of our 407th battalion. At this point I was assigned this tank and the three remaining tanks from my force and we moved to a defensive position at red point 263 at the intersection of 143rd and 162nd Armored Divisions supporting the Suez Canal crossing. We were very tired from the nonstop fighting and we had been briefed to watch for the approach of Egyptian forces which might try and smash our line. It was hard; in the desert a tank at long range is just a black dot and the situation is much worse in the dark and when you are tired. One night earlier while on alert I woke up my troops because I thought I saw Egyptian infantry approaching, but it was just a bush moving in the wind.

Yehuda Geller's battalion was also in the midst of the fighting: "As for the 410th Battalion under my command during the war, its battles were similar to those of other battalions on the Sinai front, mostly a war against infantry targets, antitank missiles, and artillery and lastly against Egyptian armored units and various antitank cannons. None of which were out of the ordinary for this type of tank."

The Israeli forces established a bridgehead over the Canal. They fought off three intense but uncoordinated counterattacks by both the Egyptian Second and Third Armies as the battle of the Chinese Farm continued on October 15–17. The 87th Reconnaissance Battalion was hit by a major attack during the early hours of October 16. It turned back the Egyptians, but at a high cost; its commanding officer Major Yoav Brom and 24 other members of the unit were killed, scores more wounded, and

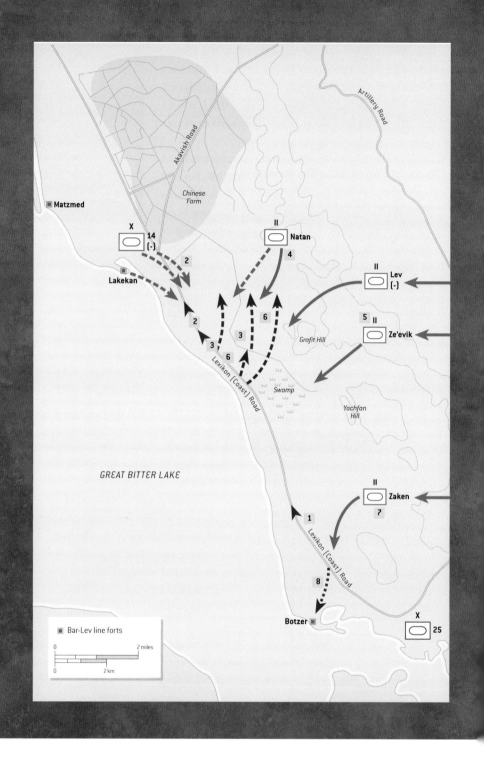

Matzmed

Akavish Road

Chinese Farm

Artillery Road

X
14
(-)

Lakekan

2

II
Natan

4

II
Lev
(-)

2

2

5 II

3
6

3

6
Grafit Hill

II
Ze'evik

Lexikon (Coast) Road

Swamp

Yachfan Hill

GREAT BITTER LAKE

II
Zaken

7

Lexikon (Coast) Road

1

8

Botzer

X
25

Bar-Lev line forts

0   2 miles

0   2 km

many of the unit's vehicles were destroyed or damaged. The following morning, Colonel Reshef, CO of the 14th Armored Brigade, met with the remaining troops of the 87th and decided to transfer the remaining tanks, APCs, and troops to other units within his brigade, where they continued to fight.

THE BATTLE OF THE CHINESE FARM, OCTOBER 17, 1973

1. Egyptian 25th Armored Brigade advances in a 16km road column up Lexikon. Israeli 14th Armored Brigade reports its approach.

2. At about 1230hrs, Egyptian advance guard probes A company near the road and Lakekan Fort. Israelis return fire. Egyptians claim losses limited to five tanks. A company, out of ammo, retires, replaced by C company (five tanks), killing eight more tanks. Egyptian advance guard retreats. 14th Armored Brigade calls artillery fire on the Egyptian column, overruled by 162nd Armored Division HQ.

3. 1430hrs – Egyptians re-launch attack up the Lexikon Road. Some tanks hit minefields near Lakekan. Natan and 14th open fire. Egyptian advance halted, a right-flank attack disrupted by partially-filled irrigation canal.

4. Lieutenant Colonel Natan's battalion (Sh'ot Cal tanks) of 460th Brigade, 162nd Armored Division, flanks the Egyptians.

5. Lieutenant Colonel Giora Lev's battalion (about 14 Magachs) and Major Ze'evik's (Magach) battalions, 600th Brigade, 162nd Division, jumping off from the Artillery Road, join the fighting about 1500.

6. 1530hrs – most remaining Egyptian AFVs are knocked out.

7. Around 1500hrs, Lieutenant Colonel Nahum Zaken's battalion, 217th Brigade moves towards Botzer (Lieutenant Colonel Eli Shimski's tank battalion of this brigade guarded its flank to the south). Zaken halts at 1700hrs. Two tanks are lost to an Israeli minefield and one to a *Sagger* ATGM. Israeli artillery hits Botzer.

8. At 1600hrs, covered by an airstrike on the 600th Armored Brigade (MiG-17s dropping napalm, one shot down), Egyptians disengage. At about 1630hrs remaining Egyptian AFVs retreat to Botzer. Reinforced by infantry, they hold Botzer until disengagement in February 1974.

A survivor of the Chinese Farm, a 25th Armored Brigade T-62 Model 1967 tank, moves back to positions near the Egyptian base at Kabrit in February 1974 as part of the post-hostilities ceasefire. (United Nations via Steven Zaloga)

Other Israeli units defeated counterattacks by the Egyptian 14th Armored Brigade, 21st Armored Division, 16th Infantry Division, and, in the climactic engagement, the 25th Armored Brigade, made up of 94 T-62 tanks and 40 BTR-50/60s APCs commanded by Colonel Ahmad Halamni Hassan. This unit advanced north on the morning of October 17 along the Lexicon (east coast) Road by the Great Bitter Lake from the Third Army defensive positions, with a goal of linking up with the 16th Infantry Division attacking from the north and cutting off the Israeli penetration. It did not deploy flank guards, but an advanced guard preceded the column. (See tactical map for details of this M60/T-62 battle.)

Ehud Gross' company had been sent forward to defeat any probes between the brigade and its objective. It was in positions between the Bar-Lev Line fort at Lakekan and the Lexicon Road, when it encountered the Egyptians:

> In the morning on October 17 my four tanks were positioned on a plateau near Great Bitter Lake. We detected the approach of the Egyptian 25th Armored Brigade equipped with their new T-62s from the south toward the north, right at us. We alerted our leaders of this fact. I was ready to act even if I only had four tanks. When they came within a range of about 2,000m we started firing for all we were worth. Due to our small number and their large force, we did not strictly follow standard Israeli doctrine of firing several shells per tank target. We just fired a shell and moved our tank and fired again to hit them and survive. In less than three minutes there were between eight and 15 of the approaching tanks burning.

The Egyptian advance guard had been defeated. The Egyptians returned fire and claim to have wiped out Gross' company, which they estimated at seven tanks. But Israeli accounts report only the possible loss of a single tank to Egyptian tanks in that engagement.

When the remainder of the Egyptian brigade attempted to advance, Gross was part of the main action:

> Colonel Reshef, our brigade commander, joined us in shooting the Egyptian tanks. This was the first time the American M60A1 and Russian T-62 fought, to my knowledge, and we had no trouble knocking out the T-62s with our 105mm guns. The Egyptians did not break in all directions to get away from our fire nor try to flank us nor did they fire more than about 10–15 shells our way before they broke off. Elements of Adan's division [Colonel Nathan Nir's 217th Armored Brigade] equipped with Centurions came in from the flank and we both continued to pound away at the 25th Brigade. My tanks were out of antitank shells and we pulled away to rearm.

The Egyptian 25th Armored Brigade had been trapped in a classic L-shaped ambush, with the Israeli tanks of the 14th Armored Brigade across their line of advance and the 217th Armored Brigade in turret-down positions on their flank inland from the flat ground on the shores of the lake. Swamps, the irrigation ditches of the Chinese Farm, and extensive Israeli minefields limited the 25th Armored

A knocked-out Egyptian T-62, probably from the 25th Armored Brigade, on the shores of the Great Bitter Lake. It may have been one of the tanks lost near the Lakekan Fort during the initial engagement. This area has now been covered by mud dredged from the Great Bitter Lake to enlarge the channel. (US DoD)

Brigade's ability to maneuver out of the trap. One Egyptian armor officer later told a British journalist: "The skies were suddenly full of red balls coming toward our tanks and many were hit and set on fire," the comment underlining the propensity of the T-62 to suffer catastrophic kills.

What was left of the Egyptian 25th Armored Brigade retreated back to the abandoned Bar-Lev Line fort at Botzer, at the junction of the Great Bitter Lake and Little Bitter Lake. The 25th Armored Brigade lost what the Israelis claimed were about 85 of 96 T-62s and all or almost all of its APCs (because the Israelis did not occupy the battlefield, they were unable to either recover Egyptian tanks or count wrecks). The brigade's surviving T-62s were put under operational command of the Egyptian 4th Armored Division for the remainder of the war. The Egyptians claimed their losses amounted to about a third of the brigade and that some had been knocked out by US-made Tube-Launched, Optically Tracked, Wire-Guided (TOW) ATGMs (which the Israelis had first used on October 14). Israeli losses amounted to four tanks, one (possibly) to tank gunfire near Lakekan Fort and three near Botzer Fort: two to maneuvering into a minefield (part of the original canal defenses) and one to a Sagger ATGM. The destruction of the 25th Armored Brigade meant that the Israeli bridgehead over the Canal was now secure.

By early on October 18, the Israelis had a bridge across the Suez Canal. The next day the roller bridge, pulled by 16 Magach tanks, was in place. Geller's 410th Armored Battalion had towed the roller bridge up to the waterway to support the crossing of the Suez Canal late on October 18: "This bridge was towed to the Canal by my battalion, carried by 16 tanks for about 7 miles, under attack by helicopters, artillery and fighter jets, over very rough ground. The main issue of the towing was to synchronize the movement of the tanks and navigation along the exact path, avoiding breaking the bridge. It took us four hours to cross those 7 miles and to bridge the two banks. The completion of the bridge had critical implications for the rest of the war."

By October 19, elements of two Israeli divisions were pouring into Africa: the 143rd Armored Division headed north, while the 162nd moved south. Tanks rolled into

many Egyptian SAM sites. By later that day, the Egyptians, who had thought the Israelis had only put a small force over the Canal, recognized the seriousness of the situation.

The Israelis had modified their tactics. Israeli tanks now fought as part of combined arms teams down to the company and battalion levels, tanks often advancing "checkerboarded" with alternating APCs. Experience of the power of Egyptian ATGM teams led to tanks carrying more HE, HEAT, and HEP and fewer APDS. Major General Emanuel Sekal (ret.) recalled that standard load in his Magach 3 unit was 24 APDS, 15 HEAT, 16 HEP, four flechette (a shotgun shell type munition firing tiny arrows that would cut ATGM wires) and four white phosphorous (to blind ATGM operators).

Fighting continued, with both sides suffering heavy losses, until October 22 when a United Nations ceasefire came into effect. The Israelis continued to advance to the Gulf of Suez, and achieved this goal late on October 23 in order to complete their encirclement of the Egyptian Third Army. Before the ceasefire, three tanks from the 87th Reconnaissance Battalion, operating with the 48th Paratroop Battalion, were hit and destroyed in heavy fighting near Ismailia, which was defended by Egyptian paratroopers armed with Sagger ATGMs and RPGs in built-up areas and irrigated farmland. With a crisis between the superpowers now overshadowing the war, fighting along the Suez Canal stopped around midnight on October 23.

After the ceasefire, the 87th Reconnaissance Battalion was reformed as part of the 143rd Armored Division with M113 APCs and jeeps equipped with TOW ATGMs (first provided to Israel by the US airlift during the war), but no tanks. Later in 1973, when the division was withdrawn from the Israeli bridgehead in Africa, the battalion ceased to exist. Sharon sent a letter after the conflict to its veterans:

> At the moment of the ceasefire, when I was standing in the outskirts of Ismailia watching the last tanks of the 87th burning, I saw before my eyes the unit's warriors as I saw them on the day of Yom Kippur. I remembered the expression of resolve on their faces, and I knew now that they had not failed. Many of them did not live to see the end of the war, but they were the men that made the end of the war possible. I have known many great battalions throughout my military career; the 87th was among the finest of them all.

IMPACT OF THE WAR

Total Israeli tank strength on the Sinai front had varied: 290 on October 6, 650 on October 10, 800 on October 15, 630 on October 22 and 570 at the ceasefire. In the Sinai, 1,450 Israeli Armored Corps (IAC) personnel were killed, 3,143 wounded, and 232 captured. Open source US postwar analysis estimated 700–1,000 total IDF tank losses. No official figures were released. As Israeli sources listed 250 tanks as being knocked out on the Golan (and 150 of those were repaired and sent back into action), the majority of the Israeli tank losses appear to have been on the Sinai front.

The value of recovery and repair for sustained combat was one of the most important lessons of the war. Effective recovery and repair capability was an Israeli strength that helped sustain the tank force levels on both fronts. Nearly all Israeli tanks were damaged in battle. Tanks not captured or totally destroyed by fire and detonation of the ammunition were reworked and returned to service or used for parts to support the repair of other tanks. A USMC study reported that the battle damage repair rates for the October 1973 war were: Centurion – 60 percent returned to action; T-54/55 – 55 percent returned to action; and M48/60 – 19 percent returned to action. That the standard US battle tank was less than one-third as likely as the earlier Centurion design to be able to go back into combat provided an alert to the US Army.

The Israelis also looked hard at the performance of all their tanks. General Adan, who remained in the job as acting head of the Armored Corps, evaluated and documented the lessons from the conflict to prepare a plan for the future. This plan

Former Syrian T-62 Model 1972 tanks at Aberdeen Proving Ground, MD. (US DoD via Steven Zaloga)

included a concept in which combat-experienced veterans "adopt" a new tank crew fresh out of training and teach them to survive on the modern battlefield. Tactics and organizations were modified to ensure that Israeli tanks would fight as part of combined arms teams. The 87th's performance led the Israelis to ensure that all armored divisions had a comparable divisional reconnaissance battalion.

The Israelis also looked at the performance of the different types of tanks. Adan himself considered the T-62's 115mm gun better than the M60's 105mm; the Israelis retained it on captured T-62s (ex-Syrian), which they put into service as the Tiran 6. Yehuda Geller said:

> I am not aware of all the advantages of the M60A1 tank over other IDF battle tanks during the war. There was a significant improvement in the front armor as compared to the M48A3, and in the turret structure, as well as various internal improvements. At the same time, the tank's main weaponry – its excellent propulsion system, and cannon and ammunition – remained as before.
>
> On the other hand, the M60A1 tank exhibited several disadvantages. One was the extra height following the addition of the small turret, but the more problematic one was the M85 machine gun located in it, and never actually fired under battle conditions. As far as it was said, the tank arrived with a defective parallel [coaxial] machine gun that was replaced by the venerable and reliable Browning 0.3in [M1919] before the war. By the way, in order to improve the force of shooting against infantry forces, Israeli machine guns were installed on top of the turrets throughout the fighting.
>
> In my personal assessment, the M60A1, the last model of the Patton, was for the most part behind its time in light of the needed technological leap to keep up with the changes that took place during the 1970s in the modern battlefield. These include the introduction of widely distributed and efficient long-range antitank guided missiles along with the personal short-range antitank rocket launchers, the various new methods of tank construction and arming, as well as the forces' formation and the operational doctrine.

Colonel Raviv's 600th Armored Brigade was the largest IDF brigade equipped with M60A1s. He said:

> No doubt the M60A1 was better equipped, easier to operate and more efficient in battle than were the Sherman, Centurion, and M48. However, the disadvantage of the M60A1 was that it would catch fire and burn easily. My experiences commanding and fighting in the Sinai led me to the conclusion that it is important that the brigade you are commanding is equipped with modern tanks, but more important is that your soldiers and crews will be motivated, experienced, well trained and they identify with the just cause of the war. If you have such soldiers even if you lose 80 percent of the brigade [113 tanks at the beginning of the war and 19 operating tanks at the end of the war and 120 crew killed] you are still considered a fighting brigade with great achievements. Both the M60A1 and T-62 are considered good tanks as the technical information has shown. As to my experience in battle between the two, the one that prevails and wins the battle will be the one with the best crew as mentioned above.

This lesson – that crew training and quality is the decisive element in armored warfare – was seen throughout the 1973 fighting. The Israelis also noted that the T-62 suffered from poor human engineering compared to the M60A1. The interior was cramped – Soviet tank crewmen were all selected from draftees under 5ft 6in (1.6m) tall – and the ride cross-country was hard and painful. In the 1973 war, numbers of Arab tankmen were affected by these conditions and some were asphyxiated or went into shock. The T-62's ethylene bromide fire extinguisher system was itself potentially lethal and the crew had to bail out if the system was triggered by a hit.

As part of the first round of Israeli analysis of the 1973 war, a senior member of the HQ staff of the 162nd Armored Division compared the different types of tanks used in the conflict:

The tanks: T-62 (115 mm gun); T-55 (100 mm gun); M60A1, M60, M48 & Centurion (105 mm gun), Super Sherman (with a French 105 mm gun). Sherman tanks with 75 mm gun and AMX-13 tanks with 75 mm gun did not take part in this war.

Firepower: The T-62 tank (with the 115 mm gun) was the only one to have an APFSDS round. This anti tank projectile has better penetration capability in RHA steel than the 105mm APDS round of the Patton (M60A1, M60, M48) and the Centurion tanks, at ranges up to 2,500m. Above this range the 105 mm APDS round has better penetration capability. The 115 mm projectile has higher muzzle velocity (about 1,600 m/sec.) but it loses about 130 m/sec per km of range (due to its large fins), whereas the 105 mm projectile has muzzle velocity of about 1450 m/sec. but it loses only about 50 m/sec. per km. Beside this the 115 mm projectile was made of relatively simple steel alloy whereas the 105 mm projectile was made of hard tungsten-carbide alloy. (The penetration capability of the 105 mm APFS projectile at 2,000 m is about 240 mm in RHA steel).

A Magach 6B Gal (a heavily modified M60A1), showing Blazer reactive armor, revised storage, smoke grenade launchers on the turret front, the Urdan low-profile cupola, and revised machine-gun (12.7mm M85 over the main gun, 7.62mm for the commander and loader) and antenna fits. It has an attachment point for engineer equipment – dozer blade or mine roller – though one is not fitted. (Steven Zaloga)

Knocked-out Israeli tanks recovered in 1973. An M48 Magach 3 is in the foreground, and an M60A1 next to it. (IDF Armored Corps Museum via Michael Mass)

The antitank round of the 105mm Sherman gun is based on a [HEAT] hollow-charge warhead and is not a kinetic projectile. Therefore it has a fixed penetration capability, regardless of range, but the overall performance of this warhead is relatively low. The T-62 and the Centurion tanks have stabilized guns whereas all the others did not. The stabilized gun improves the hit probability while on the move. The T-62, T-55 and M60A1 tank have night-vision sights based on infrared (IR) and the others did not. The T-62 and T-55 tanks have [limited] depression of their gun, up to about -6 to -7 degrees, whereas all the others have gun depression of about -10 degrees. The meaning is that in many cases the T-62 and the T-55 tanks, while in firing position (behind a fold or a small hill) did not have enough depression and so had to expose themselves more and be more vulnerable to the other side. The amount of gun rounds inside the Patton (M60A1, M60, M48) and the Centurion tanks is remarkably higher (about 60 rounds in each) than in the T-62 and T-55 tanks (less than 40 rounds). The meaning is that on average the T-62 and T-55 tanks should leave their active fight and firing positions for refilling of gun ammunition [more often] than the other tanks, which means that on average the percentage of effective tanks in each moment is smaller in T-62 and T-55 units than in the units of the other tank types.

Mobility: There is no significant difference in mobility among the above tanks, except the inferior mobility of the Sherman tank.

Armor protection: The turrets of the T-62 and T-55 tanks have better armor protection than the others, and their front and side slopes are a little bit better. The side walls of the T-62/55 are thicker than those of the various Patton tanks and the Centurion. Nevertheless the 105mm AT ammunition can penetrate almost in every point of the T-62/55 turret and hull. On the other side the T-62 with the APFSDS ammunition can penetrate the Patton and the Centurion tanks, whereas the T-55 with its [AP] antitank ammunition has some difficulties to penetrate M60 and Centurion tanks in the turret front. The Sherman tank destroyed (with the French 105 mm hollow-charge ammunition) about 40 T-62 tanks.

Survivability. The silhouette of the T-62 and T-55 tanks is smaller than [that] of the other tanks and the same is true with the silhouette of their turret. One of the most [sic] disadvantages of T-62/55 tanks is their small internal volume. The meaning is that all the internal systems are too close and when one system is hit after penetration, in most cases another system or systems are also damaged or getting out of action. Because of the small internal volume there is in the T-55 tank a fuel tank combined with gun ammunition stowage in the right front corner of the hull (I am not sure if it is the same in the T-62 tank)[it is]. The meaning is absolute destruction and explosion of the tank in case of a penetration. Analysis based up tests and war analysis showed that the improved Centurion and M60A1 were more or less on the same level survivability. Next came the M48 and Tiran 4/5 and finally the Sherman.

Reliability and human engineering. The Patton, Centurion and the Sherman tanks were better maintained by Israeli ordnance technicians under field conditions, and they succeeded in repairing many of the damaged tanks, in relatively short time, and to send them back to the armor units. As regard to human engineering the best were the Patton tanks (M60/48), then the Centurion and way behind the T-62/55 tanks. The meaning is that the crews of the Patton and Centurion tanks could fight longer periods of time without being exhausted relative to the crews in the T-62/55 tanks. The T-62/55 tanks have slightly more reliable automotive and suspension systems.

While the 1973 war was in progress, a massive supply of US armor, including hundreds of M60s, M60A1s, M113 APCs and other weapons, were stripped from war reserve stocks in Germany, the United States, and other locations and delivered to Israel by air (a few M60A1s were brought to Israel in well-publicized airlift missions by C-5A transports) or sea. Deliveries of US tanks and other ground combat weapons continued until the 1980s.

Major General Moshe "Mussa" Peled assumed the position of IAC commander in April 1974, and his team began rebuilding the force. Over time Magach and Sh'ot Cal tanks were reworked to repair battle damage and equip them with new systems to improve their utility on the battlefield. Tank commanders' under-armor optics were improved; Israeli tank commanders had fought with their heads above the turret in 1973, and suffered many casualties as a result. Other improvements included additional machine guns and 60mm mortars to counter antitank weapons, high-speed fire-suppression systems, and Blazer reactive armor (see below). The hydraulic fluid was changed and the hydraulic lines re-routed inside the turret to reduce the chance of secondary explosions.

A complete set of Blazer reactive armor weighed about 1,500kg, and the M60A1 tank set had about 42 large M2 and 49 smaller M1 explosive boxes, attached to

Lebanon, 1982. A Magach 6B (M60A1) with a partial set of Blazer armor. Some of the boxes on the turret are missing, showing the attachments. These have not been detonated – detonation would have damaged the attachment points. (Steven Zaloga).

external rails that were in turn bolted to 111 studs (these had to be welded to the turret and hull). The tank's hull and turret were covered by these metal boxes. If a box was hit by a shaped-charge warhead, such as used by an ATGM or HEAT shell, the box's fast-acting explosive would detonate outward quickly enough to counteract the warhead's explosive jet, preventing it from penetrating the tank's armor. While the armor provided tanks with extra protection, there were drawbacks to the Blazer system. Troops in close proximity were at risk when a box detonated and the boxes themselves were vulnerable to shell fragments, shock from guns firing, cross-country movement, and damage from trees and brush. Blazer could not be used on APCs as its own explosions would blow in the underlying armor.

At this time, Israel committed itself to the Merkava tank project led by General Tal, the objective being to create a new, highly survivable tank designed specifically to meet Israeli requirements. Since it took many years to design and produce enough Merkavas to fill out the frontline force, Magachs formed the backbone of the IAC from the 1973 war until the late 1990s, and they remained in service in 2009–10. When replaced by Merkavas, the newest upgraded Magachs replaced older vehicles in reserve units.

Magach 3s, based on the M48A1/A2/A3, and Magach 5s, based on the M48A5, were equipped with Blazer reactive armor and served in regular and reserve units until the 1980s. Newer M60s were upgraded as the Magach 6 received the Israeli-designed Urdan low-profile cupola. M60A1 Magach 6As had fire-control improvements added and their machine-gun cupola removed and replaced with the low profile Israeli-designed Urdan cupola. The Israelis used the M60A1 RISE (Reliability Improvement of Selected Equipment) as the Magach 6R. Several machine guns were added on the turret. They also received Blazer reactive armor.

In the 1980s, Magach tanks operating in Lebanon and the border areas began to face heavy losses to antitank missiles, mines, and roadside bombs. These losses led to a further retrofit program, as hundreds of Magach tanks received armor packages

using technology from the Merkava program, in the form of passive armor, as well as a more powerful diesel engine and upgraded transmission. These tanks were known as the Magach 6B, 6C, 7A, 7B, or 7C depending upon the armor array, fire-control suite, and other enhancements.

Magach tanks saw regular combat along Israel's borders and in Lebanon, including in the 1978 and 1982 Lebanon and 2008–09 Gaza conflicts. The 1982 Lebanon conflict saw additional M60 vs. T-62 combat. On June 10, 1982, M60s of the 211th Armored Brigade's reconnaissance battalion fought Syrian T-62s of the 85th Brigade and knocked out seven with no Israeli tank losses. The T-62 has remained in Syrian service and equipped most of the 9th Armored Division when it deployed to Saudi Arabia in 1990.

After the 1973 war, the Soviets rushed replacement tanks to Egypt, many of them T-62s. The independent tank brigades were reformed, but the Egyptian Army itself

Lebanon, 1982. A Magach 6B (M60A1 with a full set of Blazer armor) leads a column of M113 APCs. Its smoke grenade launchers are covered over by an armored box. In 1982, many Magach tanks carried orange air recognition panels on their tops and temporary recognition markings with numerals or Hebrew letters on panels. (Steven Zaloga).

41

Egyptian M60A3s of the 4th Armored Division deployed to Saudi Arabia during Operation *Desert Shield*, 1990. (US DoD photo by T/Sgt H. Deffner)

largely remained the same as when it crossed the Suez Canal on October 6, 1973. The rapid movement that led to the climactic engagement of the battle of the Chinese Farm, with the 25th Armored Brigade hurrying north along the east coast road of the Great Bitter Lake, was a rare example of Egyptian tanks reacting quickly and making a (counter) offensive move. Unlike the Soviets, the Egyptians in 1973 aimed to avoid tank-on-tank battles until Israeli tanks had been subject to attrition from Egyptian special operations forces and infantry armed with *Sagger* ATGMs and RPG-7s. When Egyptian tanks had led the attack on Israeli forces, as during the renewed offensive on October 14 or in the uncoordinated counterattacks at Chinese Farm, they did not succeed.

Following the improved Egyptian security relationship with the United States after the Camp David accords of 1979, T-62s were replaced by M60A3s. Some 750 M60A3s were transferred to Egypt by 1987 and a further 150 in 1987–93. They were issued first to the two independent tank brigades and then to the 4th and 9th Armored Divisions. As with the original T-62s, the Egyptians issued the new tanks a brigade at a time. T-62s were used to backfill the tank battalions in mechanized divisions. A range of upgrades were retrofitted to Egypt's T-62s. Most tank battalions of all types increased their strength to 31 tanks each. One of the two independent armored brigades was incorporated in the 33rd Mechanized Division when this was formed in the early 1980s. Increasingly, US models of training and tactics replaced those derived from the Soviets in the Egyptian military, just as Soviet-derived models had replaced those inherited from the British in the mid 1950s. But when the 4th Armored (with M60A3 tanks) and 3rd Mechanized Divisions deployed to Saudi Arabia in 1990, it became evident that whatever the great power model used or the nationality of their tanks' manufacture, the Egyptian Army did things their own way.

POST-1973 M60 AND T-62 DEVELOPMENT

M60 DEVELOPMENTS

The US Army paid attention to the lessons of the 1973 war. Colonel (ret.) Robert Butler, former M60 Program Manager (PM) remembers: "In the mid 1970s I went to Fort Knox to support the Tank Special Study Group which was formed to study the results of the 1973 Arab–Israeli War to determine what changes should be made to the M60 and new XM1 tank as a result of the experience gained. I was the Deputy Commander for the study group, with emphasis on the materiel requirements aspect. This very comprehensive study is still classified. Our team made recommendations for many changes to enhance US Army tank force capabilities."

The result was a large-scale re-examination of US Army operations and tactics, refocusing on the potential for a conflict in Europe. This conflict might or might not include the use of nuclear weapons, but would certainly include armored battles of greater size and duration than those of 1973, which were seen as providing insight into how Soviet numerical superiority might be countered by effective training, tactics, and technology.

One of the most perceptive observers was the combat veteran General William E. DePuy, Commander of the US Army Training and Doctrine Command (TRADOC),

A T-62 tank of the US Army at the National Training Center (NTC), Fort Irwin, California, 1985. The US Army made extensive use of T-62s at the NTC. The creation of the NTC and realistic opposing forces (OPFOR) was a critical part of the US Army's transition from its post-Vietnam state to the highly efficient force that won the 1991 war. (US DoD)

who was a leading figure in the efforts to turn the US Army around from its post-Vietnam nadir. His team created a number of reports and identified 162 improvements and updates needed to enable the US Army to fight a modern combined arms conflict based on the lessons of the 1973 war. "First, that modern weapons are vastly more lethal than any weapons that we have encountered on the battlefield before. Second, in order to cope with these weapons it is essential that we have a highly trained and highly skilled combined arms team of armor, infantry, artillery and air defense backed by the support required to sustain combat operations. Third, the training of the individual as well as the team will make the difference between success and failure on the battlefield." DePuy himself added: "Tanks and other combat elements which expose themselves during offensive action will suffer unacceptable losses unless their vulnerability can be decreased through improved tactics and techniques of movement which better use the terrain, and the application of suppressive fire of enemy anti-tank weapons. I believe that is the single most important lesson of the Arab–Israeli War."

Brigadier General John Sherman Crow was a colonel at the time, working for the chief of the US Army's Armor branch, then-Major General Donn Starry:

The doctrinal development after '73 was just as revolutionary as the combat system development… General DePuy oversaw a major rewrite of FM [Field Manual] 100-5 with General Starry himself as one of the principal authors. The TRADOC and Combat Development Center (CDC) commands picked up the 1973 Lessons Learned and began a swift Army transition. Our doctrine shifted – no more static defenses – the Active Defense Doctrine evolved by 1976… Ground combat enhancements made to US and allied forces and doctrine as a result of the 1973 war had a major influence on military tactics and the need for new systems… In 1976 an updated version of the FM 100-5 manual came out in the form of a looseleaf binder with a camouflage cover. The content reflected the themes developed by TRADOC from the 1973 war and other lessons about fire, movement, offense, and defense dating back to the Second World War known initially as active defense. This document generated significant debate about the way wars would be fought in the future and the role of armor together with other combat and support arms. Army training changed dramatically in the 1970s to reflect these concepts. This included individual and unit training and the use of the Laser MILES [Multiple Integrated Laser Engagement System] suite for more realistic combined arms combat training. Eventually the US Army created the National Training Center, where armored and mechanized units from the active and reserve force could train in a realistic environment against Opposing Force (OPFOR) units which replicated the equipment and tactics of the Warsaw Pact and forces trained and supplied by the Soviet Union. Another area of focus was the critical role of army–air force cooperation... The doctrine debate and closer ground–air cooperation eventually led to the AirLand Battle Doctrine, where a conflict was fought across the battle zone from frontline to deep rear area simultaneously using the full range of air and ground weapons to disrupt an adversaries' ability to understand the flow of battle, move effectively and control his forces.

US Army assessments rated the M60 series and the T-62 as about equal, but three M60 problems needed quick correction. First, ammunition stowage in the turret (of both the M60 and M48) caused a high percentage of catastrophic losses, with the turret being blown off. As a result, modification kits allowing ammunition for the main gun to be moved from the turret into the hull were fitted to frontline versions of the M60 series tanks. Second was that in the 1973 war the M60A1 was found to have good armor protection with the exception of the area around the chin area of the turret and around the turret ring. Penetration there would ignite the inflammable hydraulic fluid used to drive the turret, causing fires that injured the crew and could lead to ammunition detonations. To remedy this problem, an armored fillet was added to existing tanks and made a part of newly cast turrets and hulls. New non-flammable hydraulic fluid was adopted. Third, Israeli tankers, like their US counterparts, found that the 12.7mm machine-gun cupola on top of the turret did not work well and made the tank too tall.

These three issues were a priority to Colonel Butler, along with the more immediate one of making sure US tank gunfire was more effective: "We developed a number of M60 enhancements directly from the lessons of 1973 experience, such as less flammable hydraulic fluid, repositioning ammunition stowage to below the turret, addition of armor to the chin of the turret and turret ring on new M60s, and testing of a low profile cupola with a revised machine gun mount, and addition of a computer and laser rangefinder for quicker and more accurate gunnery." Butler was one of the many tankers who appreciated these post-1973 upgrades to the M60: "The top loading air cleaner, quick disconnect fuel and hydraulic lines and quick release cross-drive retainers were a blessing to our maintenance people. We could pull and replace a power pack in a fraction of the time required of the WP [Warsaw Pact tanks like the T-62]. And of course, higher flash point cherry juice [hydraulic fluid] would add to survivability. With these changes, the US Army still estimated that if a 115mm

US M60A1 GUN/TURRET

Loader's control

1. Breech operating handle, on gun mount

Gunner's controls

2. M105C telescopic sight
3. Binocular M32 periscope and battlesight
4. Gunner's switch box
5. Manual traversing locking lever
6. Ballistic shield operating handle
7. Manual traversing handle
8. Firing buttons
9. Control handles (on H-shape control wheel)
10. Firing button (alternative)
11. Manual elevating handle
12. Manual firing handle

Commander's controls

13. M17A1 rangefinder
14. Firing switch
15. Control box
16. Intercom control box
17. Commander's control handle

18. M900 HVAPFSDS round
19. M456A2 HEAT round
20. M735 HVAPFSDS round
21. M735 HVAPFSDS penetrator

APFSDS projectile penetrated an M60A1, it would have a 54 percent probability of killing it; 75 percent for HEAT."

The losses and performance of M60 series tanks in 1973 also forced a reexamination of US Army's tank capability and war reserve requirements. In the mid 1970s, the US Army's capability to fight a war in Europe depended almost exclusively on the M60. In 1976 the active duty force structure then included 2,790 M60A1s and 448 M60A2s, while the reserve force fielded 3,367 M48A3/A5s, M60s, and M60A1s. Some 3,648 tanks were listed in maintenance and war reserve status, with 2,711 of these being M60A1 tanks. The Department of Defense (DoD) and Congress ordered more rapid tank production to make up for the tanks shipped to Israel. With tank production of the M60A1 running at fewer than 40 per month (for both the US and foreign military sales), it was a shock to see that it would take several years to expand tank production due to the limited number of firms able to cast M60 tank hulls and turrets. The 1973 war clearly indicated the high rates of tank attrition to be expected in any future conflict, so it was clear that the US Army tank inventory needed to be expanded, the M60 upgraded, and XM1 Abrams tank program (to replace the M60) speeded up.

The M48A5 upgrade program upgraded more than 1,800 aging M48 tanks with 105mm cannon, AVDS-1790 diesel engine, Urdan low-profile cupola, pintle-mounted machine gun, and other enhancements. The tanks from the program equipped two active battalions in Korea, Reserve and National Guard armored units, and international customers. A program to upgrade the M60A1 was also initiated.

1983 – Georgia National Guard M60A3s of the 1-108th Armor are unloaded after an exercise at Fort Stewart. The M60A3 would remain the standard MBT of the National Guard and Army Reserve to the end of the Cold War. (US DoD)

The first step included a stabilization system for the 105mm cannon that enabled a 50 percent probability of hit while firing on the move, which 1973 combat experience had shown was effectively zero without the system. In 1977, a new version of the M60A1, with RISE and passive night sights using image intensifiers (passive infrared), entered production. T142 treads with replaceable pads replaced the earlier T97. The reliability improvements, however, proved largely marginal.

The ultimate US upgrade was the M60A3, which went into production in 1978 (both new construction and upgraded M60A1s), adding a new fire-control suite for the main 105mm cannon. The suite included a laser rangefinder, ballistic computer, a thermal sleeve for the barrel, new 7.62mm M240 coaxial machine gun (based on the FN MAG design used by Israel), and a forward-looking infrared (FLIR) tank thermal sight (TTS) that allowed effective engagement at night and in poor weather conditions, a reflection of the importance of continuous 24-hour day and night tank combat that was also a lesson of 1973.

The M60A3 was the first production tank to incorporate a TTS. While not widely publicized, the performance of this system was better than the similar sensor used on the M1. The fire-control suite in the M60A3 gave American tank crews day, night, and poor weather surveillance and a first-round hit advantage over not only the T-62, but also other tanks fielded in the 1980s. It allowed the tank commander to fight more effectively under armor, increasing his situational awareness. Another key lesson of 1973 – lack of effective night sights and night combat training would be costly – was reflected in both the investment in the TTS and in a new emphasis on night training throughout the US Army. Brigadier General Crow said:

We needed qualitative advantages in our combat systems to have a chance in NATO against a vastly superior Soviet/WP threat. Evaluation of WP weapon system effectiveness confirmed the need for a revolutionary approach to the design of the M60 follow on, the M1 Abrams. Crew protection and survivability through the application of "special armor" would certainly satisfy the "revolutionary approach" requirement. At the same time we needed to accelerate improvements to our M60 fleet – ammunition, fire control and what I still feel as revolutionary in itself, TTS add-on to the M60A3. A string of RISE (reliability improvement) initiatives were being applied throughout this period.

Colonel Butler (ret.) confirms the value of the TTS:

During the later 1970s, I went back to TACOM (Tank and Automotive Command) as a Colonel and served as the project manager for tank development. During this period we upgraded the latest version of the M60 tank. I served as the Program Manager for the M60A1 RISE Passive [indicating that it used the upgraded suspension and had a passive image intensifying infrared night-vision capability] and the M60A3 TTS (Tank Thermal Sight). The M60 TTS had a revolutionary fire-control system which provided a true night-fighting capability along with vastly improved first-round hit capability through the addition of a laser rangefinder, thermal gun shield, wind sensor and other improvements. This system was based on the requirements I and a small team had developed at Fort Knox during 1963–64 to take advantage of emerging thermal sight technology. During the M60TTS testing it became apparent the thermal system technology used for the M60TTS was superior to that employed in the M1.

As a result of lessons from the Middle Eastern wars of the 1970s, various other improvements were developed, tested, and fielded. First, the upgraded M392A2 APDS round was issued, with improvements to enhance penetration. Eventually the APDS round was replaced by the M735 series APFSDS rounds, similar in concept to the Soviet 115mm BM-6 rounds that had proved so effective fired from the T-62's smoothbore cannon. The APFSDS long rod penetrator with its higher length-to-diameter ratio, superior speed, and increased mass provided much greater delivery of kinetic energy to the target armor. To fire the long rod penetrators from the 105mm rifled gun essentially required a slipping rotating band to reduce excessive spin (to allow for fin stabilization during flight) and effective separation of the rod from the multi-piece sabot. The M900 series APFSDS round introduced stabiloy (depleted uranium) as the penetrator material (the M735 series only had a stabiloy core) and this material was also used in the follow-on M774 round. The new ammunition meant that post 1973 M60s would have an advantage over T-62s, which did not experience a comparable improvement. The Israelis designed and fielded similar rounds for their 105mm cannon – the M111 Hetz (arrow). This used tungsten steel as a penetrator material rather than stabiloy.

Initial versions of the M1 tank were equipped with the 105mm cannon and APSFDS antitank rounds. The United States, however, fitted the M1A1 with a new 120mm smoothbore cannon based on German technology. What made this weapon superior to the T-62's cannon was that computer sensors could now detect crosswinds and barrel heating (factors that could affect accuracy), and compensate for them via the fire-control computer.

Gun stabilization made accurate on-the-move firing possible. While this was developed primarily for the M1 tank, the M60A1 AOS (Add-on Stabilization) program was reflected in the RISE and M60A3 programs. The M60A3's laser rangefinder, with the flat trajectory and high velocity of improved tank ammunition, provided accuracy of 5–15m at 1,500m range. The capability provided by the laser rangefinder was demonstrated in an early 1970s field test using a stationary Belgian 90mm-armed M47, testing probability of hit against a 2.3m target by comparing a laser rangefinder against stereo coincidence (as introduced on the M48A2 and used by the M60A1) and stadia reticle (the basic battle sight of the T-62) rangefinders:

Range	500m	1,000m	2,000m
Laser	98%	86%	34%
Stereo coincidence	97%	70%	14%
Stadia reticle	98%	34.5%	4%

M60A1 105MM GUN ACCURACY AND ARMOR PENETRATION						
Range (km)	0.5	1	1.5	2	2.5	3
M728 APDS – accuracy	94%	86%	61%	44%	25%	8%
M456A2 HEAT –accuracy	89%	69%	50%	28%	17%	3%
M393 HEP –accuracy	89%	56%	47%	28%	17%	3%
M728 APDS – penetration	300mm	275mm	250mm	225mm	200mm	175mm
M456A2 HEAT – penetration	425mm	425mm	425mm	425mm	425mm	425mm

Probability of effective hit on 2.3m target. Penetration of vertical steel armor at zero-degree angle of impact. Static target and shooter, optical (non-laser) sights.

If a hit was scored, lethality was high. The US Army estimated that if it struck home a 105mm APDS, HEAT, or HEP projectile had, respectively, a 71, 75, and 81 percent chance of killing a T-62, either putting it out of action or preventing it from moving or firing.

US M60 armor also was upgraded with the Israeli Blazer system. The US Army ordered enough Blazer to equip the two tank battalions then in Korea. When these re-equipped with M1 tanks in the late 1980s, they made the armor available to the Marines, who were not scheduled to re-equip with M1s until after 1992.

T-62 DEVELOPMENTS

The T-62 also underwent a series of post-1973 upgrades that reflecting the lessons of war and the availability of improved technology. These upgrades, however, were neither as widespread nor as comprehensive as those reflected by the M60A1 RISE Passive or the M60A3. Rather, the upgrades were made incrementally and only to a part of the Soviet force structure.

The first upgrade was applied to new production T-62s starting in 1972 (preceding the 1973 war), and included the fitting of 12.7mm DShkM heavy machine guns to the turret (reflecting the increasing threat from attack helicopters) and improvements to deep wading capability. KTD-1 externally mounted laser rangefinders were added to some T-62s, starting in 1975. In the late 1970s, some Soviet T-62s were retrofitted with T-72 track and drive sprockets. Some T-62s also received engine improvements to their V-55U diesel.

T-62 M1972 GUN/TURRET

1	Tank bearing indicator	
2	Gun exhaust port	
3	Grounding for radio antenna	
4	TPN-1-41-11 5.5 power infrared monocular periscope and gunsights.	
5	TNP-165 1-power vision block	
6	TSh2B-41u gunner's telescopic sight	
7	Optical filter	
8	Gunnery table	
9	Gun electric switch	
10	Main gun breech	
11	Gun elevation level	
12	Searchlight control	
13	NBC system control	
14	breach mechanism manual handle	
15	Loader's MK-4 periscope	
16	breech mechanism, 7.62mm PKT co-axial machinegun	
17	co-axial MG power source	
18	solenoid for co-axial machinegun	
19	electric trigger for co-axial machinegun	

20	TPU tank intercom plug-in
21	co-axial mechanism and ammunition feed tray
22	Ready ammunition racks
23	Automatic sliding breech block
24	Projectile tray
25	Gunner's leg shield
26	Gun control – ammunition type
27	Gun switches
28	Manual gunlaying equipment
29	BR-5 HVAPFSDS round
30	BM-6 HVAPFSDS penetrator
31	BK-4M HEAT round

In the early 1980s, the T-62M upgrade package featured appliqué multilayer laminated armor on the turret. Other armor enhancements included hinged side skirts, lightweight hull and rear turret armor against RPG warheads, and under-belly armor

A US Army T-62 demonstrates the tank's ability to create a smokescreen by heating diesel fuel in its engine exhausts. The M60 series has a similar capability, but during the 1991 Gulf War tanks running on JetA fuel were unable to do this (US DoD)

OPPOSITE TOP
A USMC M60A1 RISE Passive with Blazer armor in Exercise *Solid Shield* at Camp Lejeune in 1989, one of the few pre-*Desert Shield* opportunities for the Marines to gain familiarity with the system. (US DoD photo by SSgt. S. Stewart)

against antitank mines. A version with the full range of armor upgrades, unofficially designated T-62E, saw extensive combat in Afghanistan. The upgraded Tucha 82mm smoke grenade launcher system was fitted. The improved KTD-2 laser rangefinder was matched to an improved BV-62 ballistic computer, gunner's sight, and gun stabilization system. A thermal sleeve was added to the gun barrel. Some of the 750-plus T-62Ms were fitted with a capability to fire the 9K116-2 Bastion (NATO codename: AT-10 *Stabber*) antitank guided missile, which was loaded like a standard 115mm round and fired down the tank barrel, using laser beam-riding guidance. Some T-62Ms also received the versions of the V-46 diesel engine developed for the T-72. A number of T-62Ms and other upgraded T-62s were also fitted with *Reaktion* explosive bricks, a Soviet version of the Blazer system, and an improved NBC defense filtration system.

Post-Soviet Russia has used T-62s in fighting in Chechnya and also in Georgia (where it has also been used by the Georgian Army).

T-62 115MM MAIN GUN ACCURACY AND ARMOR PENETRATION						
Range (km)	0.5	1	1.5	2	2.5	3
BR-5 APFSDS – accuracy	98%	79%	50%	27%	14%	8%
BK-4M HEAT – accuracy	89%	69%	33%	11%	3%	3%
APFSDS – penetration	350mm	300mm	285mm	270mm	245mm	215mm
HEAT – penetration	430mm	430mm	430mm	430mm	430mm	430mm
Effective hit on 2.3m target. Penetration of vertical steel armor at zero-degree angle of impact. Static target and shooter. Optical (non-laser) sights.						

USMC M60A1 vs. IRAQI T-62, KUWAIT 1991

In the years after 1973, M60s and T-62s saw action in conflicts throughout the Middle East and South Asia. In the Iran–Iraq War (1980–88), Iranian M60s and Iraqi T-62s fought each other as part of large and bloody battles little known or understood in the West. The Iranian Army received 460 M60A1 tanks and these formed the backbone of several mechanized and armored divisions. Iranian M60s – primarily used in small

Iran made extensive use of M60A1s in the Iran–Iraq War. With indigenous and imported upgrades, these remain in service in 2010. Here are Iranian Army M60A1s (probably from the 3rd Battalion/81st Armoured Brigade) with infantry (probably from 7th Infantry Brigade) during Operation *Bazy Deraz*, east of Qasr-e-Shirin, in April 1981. (Via Tom Cooper)

units in an infantry support role – fought in the many armored engagements of the war. The Soviet Union used T-62s throughout what became its last war, in 1979–89 in Afghanistan. US Marine Corps M60A1s saw combat in Beirut in 1982–83 as part of the international force there. A platoon of Marine M60A1s took part in the US intervention on the Caribbean island of Grenada in 1983, but was not required to go into action.

DESERT SHIELD

The Gulf War of February 1991 brought the M60A1 and the T-62 into combat again. The context was a massive international effort to reverse the Iraqi invasion of Kuwait, which had occurred in August 1990. To oppose the Iraqi military, whose armor included T-62s, a coalition army was put together around a backbone of US forces. The USMC, Egyptian, and Saudi armored formations included M60 tanks, and this vehicle ended up playing a major role in the liberation of Kuwait, including defeating T-62s in the only battles in which US M60s confronted their Cold War counterparts.

An Iraqi Army T-62 during the Iran–Iraq War, 1986, showing tricolor camouflage. The Iraqi tankers wear standard Soviet-issue tank helmets and cotton uniforms rather than tank suits. (Tom Cooper Collection)

At the time of the invasion of Kuwait, the M60 was largely replaced by the M1 Abrams in the US Army's active force structure. The M60 continued in service with the Army Reserve and National Guard, in reserve stocks and with training units. Among these was the 2nd Battalion, 69th Armor (2-69th), and the two four-tank platoons of D Troop, 4th Cavalry, both part of the 197th Infantry Brigade, whose

1991 – US AND IRAQI TACTICAL TANK ORGANIZATION

Marine tanks in Kuwait used the same organization as US Army M60 units: five M60 tanks made up a platoon, three platoons plus two HQ tanks (one with a dozer blade) made up a 17-tank company (plus support units). While army battalions had three companies and three battalion HQ tanks (54 tanks) plus supporting units (including a self-propelled 4.2in mortar unit and a scout platoon), Marine Corps active tank battalions had 70 tanks (four companies plus two HQ tanks) and also controlled all the division's TOW ATGMs. Iraqi Army tanks units were based on Soviet models. Army companies were made up of three (four in the Republican Guards) three-tank platoons plus two HQ tanks, though few, if any, were at full strength when the ground war opened. Battalions (designated armored regiments by the Iraqis) had two HQ tanks. T-62s were often used as company and battalion command tanks in units equipped with T-55s or Chinese Type 59 tanks.

In Saudi Arabia during Operation *Desert Shield*, USMC M60A1 RISE Passive "Fat Elvis 2" – the name stenciled on the bore evacuator – has received its Blazer armor, but has not yet been painted in the desert sand color scheme. Sandbags were often used to fill gaps between Blazer boxes. (US DoD)

normal duty was training troops at Fort Benning, Georgia. Their operational role was to join the 24th Infantry (Mechanized) Division, based at Fort Stewart, Georgia, if it was ever called upon to deploy to the Middle East as part of a Central Command (CENTCOM) contingency (if the division deployed to Europe, they would take instead a National Guard brigade with M1 tanks). When the 24th became the first US-based "heavy" division to deploy to Saudi Arabia after the invasion of Kuwait, the cavalry and a few of the 2-69th's M60A3s came with them by fast sealift. The M60A3s took part in the defensive operations of Operation *Desert Shield*, but were replaced with M1A1s before Operation *Desert Sword* liberated Kuwait. The tanks themselves were turned over to the Marines, who used them to supplement their M60A1s, with tank companies in the 1st and 3rd Tank Battalions each receiving one.

On "Leatherneck Range" Marine tankers of the 3rd Tank Battalion got their first opportunity to do live fire with APFSDS rounds. The instructor is holding an M900A1 round. Because of this munition's high velocity and flat trajectory, it requires a target range with more space than is available in Marine training areas in the continental United States. The Marine tanks needed also to zero and boresight their weapons with this projectile. (US DoD photo by Sgt. D.E. Renner)

The US Air Force (USAF) deployed a handful of M60A3s from Europe to bases in Saudi Arabia and the Gulf. These tanks were acquired by the Air Force in the 1980s and used for the unexploded ordnance (UXO) mission, either shooting explosive devices or pushing them out of the way with a dozer blade.

The USMC was armed with M60A1 RISE Passive as their primary MBT. In 1985, they had 716 of these tanks, equipping three active and two reserve tank battalions, three battalion sets on Maritime Prepositioning Ships (MPS), plus war reserve and training tanks. The Marines had been reluctant until 1985 – years after the Army – to invest in the M1 with its larger size and weight (a drawback for amphibious operations and beach crossing) and its gas turbine engine, which limited its ability to wade ashore. The 105mm gun had HE and canister rounds that the M1's 120mm lacked. Dismounted infantry and engineers could more easily work with the M60A1, which had an external telephone attached to the intercom system and lacked a turbine exhaust, which kept troops from following close behind. As a result, the M1 was just being prepared to enter Marine Corps service in 1990.

The Iraqi invasion of Kuwait on August 2, 1990, brought the Marines to Saudi Arabia and, within days, M60A1s to arm them. Marine tankers from the 1st Tank Battalion, based at Camp Lejeune, North Carolina, flew to the Saudi Arabian port of Dhahran, where they "married up" with ships from the MPS. This force of merchant ships carrying tanks and heavy equipment, created in the 1980s, was intended to provide a rapid deployment capability for the USMC. By August 17, 33 Marine M60A1s were unloaded at Dhahran. They were soon joined by the 3rd Tank Battalion and, in the words of Lieutenant Colonel Alphonso Diggs, the commanding officer of the 3rd, "two Marine tank battalions faced two mechanized and one armored Iraqi divisions poised in Kuwait." But the great fear of August 1990 – that Iraq's tanks would keep rolling until they reached Saudi Arabia's port and oil fields – never materialized.

A company of Marine 1st Tank Battalion M60A1 RISE Passives fire their main guns on "Leatherneck Range" soon after arriving in Saudi Arabia in September 1990 as part of Operation *Desert Shield*. Only some of them have received hasty desert camouflage and none have yet received the attachment points for Blazer armor. The company has ring barrel markings around the main gun as a recognition sign. (US DoD photo by Sgt. D.E. Renner)

Tanks are dangerous even when they are not shooting. This USMC M60A1 of Company B, 3rd Tank Battalion, rolled over on its turret while being offloaded from a transporter truck during Operation *Desert Shield* in September 1990. The M88 recovery vehicle will pull it upright. The unusual position shows the T142 track's removable track pads. (US DoD photo by SSgt M. Masters)

Major General James M. "Mike" Myatt, commanding general of the 1st Marine Division, noted of this phase of the deployment: "The M60A1 tanks we got from the MPS ships were new and had never been fired before. First, we had to test fire those tanks and, second, we had to become familiar with the discarding sabot ammunition that our Marines had never been allowed to fire. By 16 September we had fired our weapons on Leatherneck Range." Such vital live-fire gunnery was all too rare during Operation *Desert Shield*. Tanks mainly fired to boresight and zero their main guns. There was relatively little opportunity for combined arms training.

The Iraqi Army's T-62s were concentrated in the armored and mechanized divisions and were also used as command tanks in units equipped with T-55 and Chinese-built T-59 (a version of the T-54) tanks. T-72s were used by the elite Republican Guard Divisions and the 12th Armored Brigade of the 3rd Armored Division. While Iraqi unit organizations and tactics were based on Soviet models, they had evolved in combat during the Iran–Iraq War to a more limited and sustainable local version of

Some of the crew of "Lefty," a USMC M60A1 RISE Passive with Blazer armor, manage to nap on folding cots (carried on the tank) while the powerpack is removed for maintenance in Saudi Arabia in February 1991. (US DoD photo by CWO2 Bradley)

Iraqi T-62 of the 3rd Armored Regiment, 6th Armored Brigade, 3rd Armored Division, identified by divisional markings of a yellow bore evacuator with a white stripe and the white-yellow-white tricolor bar on the turret sides and hull front. This tank was captured by Company A of the 8th Tank Battalion, US Marine Corps Reserve, equipped with M60A1 RISE Passives. (US DoD)

such models. Rather than making deep-penetration advances – some 35km a day, once a breakthrough had been made – as Soviet tank divisions were intended, Iraq's armored divisions were defensive, moving to sectors of the front threatened by Iranian offensives. (Iraq could afford enough tank transporter trucks to move all its tanks.) There they would halt any penetrations, either acting as mobile pillboxes in pre-constructed revetments or with effective, pre-planned, but limited counterattacks.

Spearheading the invasion of Kuwait and now occupying it were the T-62s of the Iraqi 3rd Armored Division, "Saladin", named for the great Kurdish hero who, like the division, had started out from Kirkuk. The formation had the longest combat history of any Iraqi division: it had been in Jordan during the 1967 Arab–Israeli War, in Syria during the 1973 war, and had fought throughout the Iran–Iraq War. On paper or in overhead reconnaissance photographs, with hundreds of tanks, this veteran division was a formidable force. The reality was different. Saddam Hussein's army was bigger than Iraq could support, and in the years since the Iran–Iraq War there had not been enough resources for realistic training or to create effective leaders or technicians to use and sustain the force. The 3rd Armored Division had little opportunity for gunnery training, the most important single skill for any tank crew.

While T-62s of the 3rd Armored Division's 6th Armored Brigade had been among the forces that had, with heavy losses, probed coalition forces near Wafrah, Saudi Arabia, on January 29, 1991, most of the division dug itself in to survive air attacks. Other Iraqi armor attempted a spoiling attack on coalition forces that led to the battle of Khafji, which opened on the night of January 29. According to Marine reconnaissance teams, the initial Iraqi attack by the 5th Mechanized Division, backed up by 3rd Armored Division, was led by an M60A1 tank, presumably captured from Iran.

The counterattack that finally pushed the Iraqis out of Khafji included the M60A3-equipped 7th and 8th Battalions of the Royal Saudi Land Forces' 8th Mechanized Brigade. The Saudi M60A3s had experienced serviceability problems earlier in

Operation *Desert Shield* – some 60 percent of one battalion was immobile as a result of sand-clogged air filters after its first move out of garrison into the desert. By the time of the Khafji battle, however, extensive maintenance by support personnel (largely foreign contractors) and additional training for the Saudi tank crews had improved performance. Saudi M60A3s engaged and knocked out a number of Iraqi T-59 tanks without loss.

The coalition task now became one of preparing for the liberation of Kuwait. Saddam Hussein had shown every sign of aiming to make Kuwait's annexation stick, with large-scale development of field fortifications and minefields along the border with Saudi Arabia. Iraqi general Raad Hamdani here describes the mine defenses Iraq learned to put in place in the Iran–Iraq War:

> Say a minefield was 600m wide; we would have one mine for every meter. These were the standards of usual minefields. Then, we intensified them in such a way that there were ten possibilities for a soldier to be injured by a mine along the 600m. There would be different kinds of mines: tank mines, vehicle mines, and individual mines – and we started using the Italian bounding mines, which would explode with the maximum amount of damage. We also increased the protection weapons for the minefields, like machine guns. Increased fire would stop the potential for infiltration.

Such defenses made adaptation of the M60s important, both to deal with the field fortifications and the increased opposition expected behind them.

The first adaptation was fitting the Israeli-designed Blazer reactive armor kits to Marine M60A1s. The Marines had adopted the Blazer in the 1980s after seeing its use by Israeli M60s in the 1982 war. Half of the M60A1s that had been on board MPS ships had not received the attachment points for the Blazer boxes before being landed, and these had to be modified in-theater. The remainder of the Marine M60A1s, plus the Army's few M60A3s, arrived with their Blazers. But there were not enough to go around. The 8th Tank Battalion, the last Marine tank unit to arrive in theater, had only enough boxes to defend their turret mantlets and were forced to create dummy boxes for their hulls. Many of the Marine tankers were unfamiliar with the system.

Other protection issues were not dealt with as easily. The Iraqis were known to have a large offensive chemical warfare capability and had made extensive use of it against the Iranians and their own Kurdish population. The M60A1's lack of an overpressure and filtration defensive system – something that had been identified as a requirement for future tanks back in the 1957 ARCOVE study – became a source for concern.

The most significant adaptations related to breaching the minefields and prepared defenses that the Iraqis had put in place along the Kuwaiti border. Marine M60A1s had always been equipped and their crews trained to deal with beach defenses, including minefields, but now they found themselves having to deal with a greatly expanded threat. Marine M60A1 units trained and rehearsed extensively in minefield breaching, some to the exclusion of other tasks. The tanks were fitted with increased numbers of engineer attachments. The standard M9 dozer blade, for example, had been in inventory pre-war. It was soon augmented by a full-width mine rake that plowed the ground ahead of the dozer blade. As an interim measure, the 1st Tank Battalion designed "Roller Dude," a version of a mine roller that would detonate any mines ahead of the tracks. A number of these were produced in-theater by US Navy Construction Battalion ("Seabee") personnel. Later, Israeli-produced mine rollers were used. Other M60A1s used the Mk 54 and Mk 58 (trailer mounted) mine-clearing line charges (MCLC), backing up larger versions fired from amphibious vehicles. Major General Myatt said that "We had what we needed in terms of the explosive line charges. The difficulty was that some of the mines cannot be exploded by a

1ST MARINE DIVISION, 3RD TANK BATTALION, 1991 GULF WAR (OVERLEAF)

A USMC 3rd Tank Battalion M60A1 RISE Passive with Blazer armor (specifically tank C-52 "Genesis II" of Captain Ed Dunlop, commanding officer, C Company), passes an abandoned T-62 number "21" of the Iraqi 2nd Armored Regiment, 6th Brigade, 3rd Armored Division on February, 26, 1991, the third day of the ground war. The sky is dark and overcast, with the burning oilfields to the south casting a pall rather than creating pitch darkness (as they did during the M60/T-62 battle at the Al Burqan oilfield on the morning of the second day of the war). The terrain is flat and sandy, as is most of Kuwait. The M60A1 is advancing in the tracks of a tank ahead of it to avoid landmines. The T-62 has not been hit, as the 3rd Tank Battalion, unlike the 1st, would not blow up abandoned tanks that the thermal sights of TOW-equipped HMMWVs showed were "cold."

Once deployed in 1990, USMC M60A1s acquired a new set of black tactical markings on their overall sand color scheme. Companies were indicated by chevrons: forward pointing for Company A, aft pointing for Company B, upward pointing for Company C, and downwards pointing for Company D. In some units, company commanders were indicated by a double chevron (Genesis II had such markings at some time, but not during the ground war in Kuwait). Platoons were originally identified by one, two, or three dots inside the chevron, but by the time the additional armor was fitted, this system was replaced by one, two, or three black bands on the main gun muzzle in some units, including the 8th Tank Battalion. Tank names were often stenciled in black on the main gun barrel evacuator. The Marines' 3rd Tank Battalion stenciled their scorpion battalion insignia in black on the hull rear or forward left fender. TF Papa Bear added their bear paw print insignia to the vehicle's rear. Kill markings were added to the gun barrels in some units after the shooting stopped. Many tanks flew large US national flags during the final advance into Kuwait as recognition signs; to this were added smaller Marine Corps and state or commonwealth flags on some tanks.

Immediately before the ground war opened, Marine tanks were fitted with infrared recognition lights that could be fitted to the turret rear. Many tanks carried international orange air recognition panels. Tanks carrying forward observers or forward air controllers were modified to have an externally mounted TOW sight and a laser target designator.

Most Iraqi tanks in 1991 were overall sand. This one is in a two-tone camouflage. The 3rd Armored Division had a unique unit marking created by painting the bore extractor chrome yellow with a white stripe. Many of its tanks also had a tricolor flash on the turret or hull sides and lower hull back and front. The numerals "21" are not Arabic, but rather the Hindi-style numerals used in some Arab countries. The other markings are the white-black-white tricolor unit insignia on the turret sides (forwards). This particular tank (and some but not all of the division's other vehicles) had had two stylized Arabic letters added over the insignia (initials of a slogan linking Saddam Hussein to historic Arab victories).

In Saudi Arabia during Operation *Desert Shield*, a USMC M60A1 RISE Passive (with an M9 dozer blade) of the 2nd Marine Division's TF Breach Alpha rehearses gapping the berm that the Iraqis had built along the border with Kuwait. The vehicle is equipped with Blazer armor and has its smoke grenade launchers secured under a protective covering. (US DoD photo by SSgt. M. Masters)

sympathetic detonation, these must be mechanically breached. Some of the equipment came in late. We put the track-width mine plows on our tanks."

The Iraqi reliance on antitank ditches gave additional importance to the M60-series Armored Vehicle Launched Bridge (AVLB), which is capable of bridging (in two minutes) a 13m gap. Also used was the Israeli-made Towed Assault Bridge (TAB), which was towed behind a tank and allowed 10m gaps to be crossed. While the US Army divisions did not use any M60 tanks, other M60 series vehicles – AVLBs, the M728 Combat Engineering Vehicle (CEV), and the AVLM (Armored Vehicle Launched MCLC, an AVLB chassis carrying two MCLCs) – saw widespread use.

The powerpack of "Lefty," a USMC M60A1 RISE Passive with Blazer armor, has been removed and is being worked on under field conditions in Saudi Arabia in February 1991. The old-style M60 series tanks imposed a heavy maintenance burden, compounded by an around-the-world supply line. (US DoD photo by CWO2 Bradley)

The need to have M60A1s breach the minefields throughout the USMC sector meant they had to operate away from the sea and sources of spare parts. It proved difficult to sustain the aging tanks. While the M60A1 normally ran on Diesel Fuel-2, the logistics systems delivered only JetA, leading to power loss and clogged filters in M60A1s deployed by sealift (those on the MPS ships had already been "tuned" to JetA). Few spare parts were available. Cannibalization was routine. At least one tank went into combat with an inoperable fire-control computer. "We are constantly, constantly repairing the tank," said Marine Sergeant Nelson Carter.

DESERT STORM

On February 24, when the ground war of Operation *Desert Storm* was launched, three Marine Corps M60A1 battalions crossed the border into the "heel" of Kuwait. The 1st and 3rd Tank Battalions supported the 1st Marine Division, which was driving on Kuwait International Airport. The 1st Marine Division would attack with its mechanized combined arms teams – Task Forces (TFs) Ripper and Papa Bear– led by tanks, with the light armored vehicles (LAVs) of TF Shepherd available for screening or reconnaissance and the infantry of TFs Taro and Grizzly carrying out night infiltration and air assaults as required.

To their right flank, further into the desert, the M60A1s of the 8th Tank Battalion, a Marine Corps Reserve unit three companies strong, were tasked to support the 6th Marines, advancing on the right flank of the 2nd Marine Division, along with the M1A1-equipped 2nd and 4th (-) Tank Battalions. The 2nd Marine Division was also reinforced by the US 2nd Armored Division's Tiger Brigade with two additional M1A1 battalions, forming a total of 183 M1A1s and 64 M60A1 tanks.

Two additional M60A1-equipped companies of the 4th Tank Battalion (also reservists) waited on warships in the Gulf, poised to launch an amphibious invasion if required. A total of 277 Marine M60A1 tanks were deployed for *Desert Storm*. But more important than their numbers was the role they would be playing. The Marines were leading with their tanks and would rely on them to breach the Iraqi defenses and then to enable the advance against the Iraqi's combined arms forces.

USMC M60A1 RISE at dusk in the desert, its silhouette altered by external equipment and antennas. (US DoD photo)

Iraqi T-62 captured in Kuwait in 1991, serial 20129, of the 1st Regiment, 6th Armored Brigade, 3rd Armored Division. (Roddy de Normann via Stephen Sewell)

The breaching operations commenced, with M60A1s with plows or rakes leading the advance into each breach – there were 14 in the 1st Marine Division and six in the 2nd Marine Division sectors. As the big line charges detonated, fired from Amphibious Assault Vehicles (AAVs), the tanks went forward, firing their own line charges. Line charges often failed to detonate automatically, and tankers or engineers had to fuze and fire them manually. When the line charges finally exploded, a tank went over the blast area looking for surviving mines and using an automatic lane-marking device on the rear of the tank to indicate a clear path. The tanks slowly advanced, followed by NBC reconnaissance teams, looking for signs of chemical mines.

M60A1s that had completed their breaches were diverted to help in adjacent ones. In the 1st Marine Division sector, an M60A1 with a "Roller Dude" attachment was knocked out while "proofing" a lane. In the 2nd Marine Division sector, seven M60A1s were knocked out breaching the minefields. One M60A1's mineplow, damaged by an explosion, wrapped around its treads, the disabled tank blocking the breach until it could be towed back. Two other M60A1s were knocked out by British-produced bar mines, captured from Kuwait in 1990. But the tanks and the engineers they were supporting were able to complete the breaches in less time than had been planned.

The Iraqi infantry divisions holding the frontline were supposed to delay and disrupt the coalition advance through the minefields and provide time for combined arms forces to launch pre-planned counterattacks. Weakened by the air offensive and a stretched supply line, however, they collapsed in minutes. Crowds of prisoners delayed the Marines more than resistance when clearing and expanding the breaches.

The first M60A1 action when through the minefield was a friendly fire incident. Tanks of TF Ripper – A Company, 1st Tank Battalion – engaged a truck convoy from TF Grizzly that had penetrated an adjacent breach ahead of them. Some 55 rounds of main gun ammunition killed a Marine and knocked out two trucks and an AAV. Subsequent M60A1 friendly fire incidents were less deadly. On at least two occasions, Marine M60A1s engaged AAV-7s at ranges of up to 2,000m. Fratricide became a major concern, reducing tactical maneuver during the day and keeping the Marines from advancing during hours of darkness.

For the rest of the first day of the ground war, the Marine tanks led the attack into Kuwait. The 1st and 3rd Tank Battalions encountered small units of Iraqi tanks, including T-62s, which they knocked out without loss. 1st Lieutenant William Delaney was commanding 1st Platoon, D Company, 3rd Tank Battalion from an ex-197th Brigade M60A3 in front of TF Ripper. "In all, our company got 15 tanks. It was unbelievable. Tanks blew up with tremendous explosions. Turrets flipped off. There would be 15 to 20 more explosions as ammo cooked off. Everybody in my platoon got a tank kill."

A USMC M60A1 RISE Passive – part of 2nd Marine Division's TF Breach Alpha – equipped with mine plows and a roller in position to lead a column of AAV-7 amphibious assault vehicles into a minefield breach when the ground war begins. The tank carries an air recognition panel on its turret roof. (US DoD photo by SSgt M. Masters)

The M60A1s were advancing into a relatively flat desert with only oil facilities to break up the lines of sight – open vision routinely ran to more than 5,000m, the effective maximum range for detecting a moving tank with the naked eye. Gently rolling slopes provided skillfully positioned tanks with the ability to set up hull-down engagements (with the hull protected by terrain) at ranges of 300–800m, but few of the Iraqi tanks were positioned to take advantage of these positions.

A pre-planned counterattack by the 8th Mechanized Brigade of the Iraqi 3rd Armored Division hit M1A1 tanks in the 2nd Marine Division sector and was destroyed without loss, while the M60A1s of the 8th Tank Battalion destroyed other Iraqi tanks. By the time the 3rd Armored Division's T-62s were in position to open fire against the advancing Marines, they were in much worse shape than when they had invaded Kuwait. Even during the Iran–Iraq War, 50 percent operational readiness was considered good. The air campaign had first interdicted their lines of communication – Iraqi armored forces relied on depots at Baghdad and Basra for all but the simplest maintenance – cutting off supplies and spare parts, and then started to attrite the T-62s dug into their revetments. Up to half of the division's tanks had been knocked out, although coalition planners, poring over intelligence reports, could only guess at its effects.

Covering the battlefields in Kuwait was a pall of dense smoke from the oil fields the Iraqis had set on fire. The reduced visibility materially handicapped Iraqi tank crews due to their reliance on Soviet night-vision equipment. But in the close-range tank battles that dominated in the Marines' sectors, this technology was not as decisive as it was out in the open desert. The engagements were mainly at close range, where the T-62's 115mm gun was at its most accurate and deadliest. Yet every time M60A1s and T-62s fought, superior training determined the outcome; the Marines shot first and

An abandoned Iraqi T-62 of the 2nd Regiment, 6th Armored Brigade, 3rd Armored Division in Kuwait, 1991. It is identified by the divisional markings of a yellow-painted bore evacuator with a white stripe and the tricolored flash under the hull that identifies the brigade and battalion's position in it. (Roddy de Normann via Stephen Sewell)

A captured Iraqi T-62 in 1991, from the 2nd Regiment, 6th Armored Brigade, 3rd Armored Division (tactical number 33A). Its searchlights are protected by armored mountings. (Roddy de Normann via Stephen Sewell)

hit first, without exception. Few vehicles involved in the Iraqi counterattacks survived, and none were able to hit a Marine tank.

In the afternoon of the first day, the 3rd Tank Battalion encountered more T-62s, some moving, others dug into revetments, as it moved to envelop Al Jaber airfield; all were knocked out without losses. 2nd Lieutenant James D. "Gonzo" Gonsalves, Company C, 3rd Tank Battalion, encountered a T-62 near Al Jaber airfield in the fading daylight. "We had pulled up to our second [of the] day's objective and were awaiting further orders. The smoke clouds from the burning oil wells were closing in fast, reducing visibility to less than 1,500 meters. All of a sudden my loader, Lance Corporal Rodrigues, yelled: 'We got a T-62 out there – look!'" Gonsalves gave the correct fire command: "Gunner, sabot, tank, range 1,100 meters." The 105mm fired and "the first explosion was small but then its ammo started cooking off. I counted 14 secondary explosions."

The second day of the ground war opened with a reinforced Iraqi battalion making what was termed "the reveille counterattack" against the 2nd Marine Division's right flank; M1A1s helped destroy all 39 tanks and APCs without loss. At the same time, the Iraqi counterattack at the Al Burqan oilfields on the morning of the second day of the ground war produced the most intense tank battle of the entire war. It was also the one where the odds were the most even. Visibility was close to zero and the M60A1's infrared systems were less useful among the burning oilfields.

Though this counterattack was preplanned and rehearsed, the Iraqis could not make it work. Signal intercepts and prisoner reports made it clear the attack was coming. The commanding officer of one of the lead battalions in the counterattack had surrendered with his command staff, and tried to arrange for the remainder of the battalion to be taken prisoner rather than be destroyed.

The Iraqi operation consisted of a pincer movement that jumped off at 0710hrs after moving into assembly areas overnight, and included the 8th Armored Brigade of the 3rd Armored Division. One pincer was hit by fires from five battalions of Marine artillery at about 0815hrs. Within 15 minutes TF Papa Bear received a radio report "T-62s everywhere, scattering like cockroaches from the Burqan oil field."

Major General Myatt at the 1st Marine Division found himself in the frontline as the Iraqi tanks rolled toward his forward command post (CP). "We were counterattacked at my command post by an Iraqi mechanized infantry brigade… The radio operators rolled up the sides of the tent so they could actually see where the action was – about 300 meters from my CP."

The 1st Tank Battalion had taken up a night position to the north of the Al Burqan oil fields, ready to spearhead 1st Marine Division's advance on Kuwait City in the morning, when the message came at about 0800hrs that the division's right flank was under attack from the east. Lieutenant Colonel Michael M. Kephart, commanding the battalion, would have to turn front to flank and hit the counterattacking Iraqis.

He called his company commanders together for a quick briefing before launching the attack. Just after issuing orders, the briefing was brought to a conclusion by streams of Iraqi tracer fire. An attack by the 22nd Brigade of the Iraqi 5th Mechanized Division had hit the Marine tanks. As the company commanders ran back to their commands, the tanks' supporting Marine infantry, Company I of the 3rd Battalion, 9th Marines, broke the point of the Iraqi armored thrust with accurate close-range fire from their Dragon ATGMs and handheld antitank weapons.

The M60A1s of C and D Companies of the 1st Tank Battalion joined in the defense. Dense smoke reduced visibility to less than 500m, in places to less than a tenth of that. In contrast to the one M60A3 (with thermal sights) per company, the M60A1s' passive infrared was limited to 500m or less, with the oil fires effectively providing camouflage for the Iraqis. (The HMMWV-mounted TOW launchers could detect Iraqi tanks some 4,000m away.) 2nd Lieutenant Michael Richardson heard over the company radio net: "White One, this is White Five. There's a tank right in front of you." The reply was "Well shoot it!" The first shot hit and killed the Iraqi tank. More US tanks joined in the firing. Other M60A1s had to hold fire and not maneuver

On February 25, 1991, the second day of the ground war, two Marine tank crewmen from the 3rd Tank Battalion review the maps of the day's planned advance. (US DoD photo by LCpl R. Price)

A T-62 of the Iraqi 3rd Armored Division (identified by its yellow bore evacuator with white stripe) knocked out in Kuwait near Ali-al-Salem airfield. It had been dug in to cover the suspension and put under camouflage netting, the remains of which can be seen. The use of construction material under the gun barrel is to prevent the muzzle blast disturbing sand, which would then blind the gunner until it settles. (US DoD)

to the flanks of the attack tanks due to the danger of fratricide, giving the Iraqis a numerical advantage. The M60A1s halted the Iraqi advance; they were joined, as the fog started to clear, by long-range fire from TOWs mounted on HMMWVs. Marine attack helicopters and tactical aircraft also went into action, these adding to the

T-62 IN M60A1 SIGHTS

destruction started by the Marine tanks. Fortunately, the previous day's advance over flat terrain had allowed the M60A1s to keep their battlesights zeroed rather than being jolted out of alignment. This meant that the US tank gunnery techniques, reflecting the lessons of 1973, enabled the Marines to shoot first and hit the opposing Iraqi tanks first every time.

As the Iraqi attack ground to a halt, it was time for the 1st Tank Battalion's M60A1s to go on the offensive, with Company C on the left (northern) flank and Company D on the right. The TOWs were ordered to cease fire and were pulled back to guard the left flank to prevent fratricide as the M60A1s went forward into a successful counterattack. Company C alone destroyed 18 enemy vehicles. At 1015hrs, the

The M60A1 has two gunsights, the M17A1 stereo coincidence rangefinder that provides the optical long-range fire control, and the M32 day-and-night eight-power telescopic sight, which includes the battlesight and is used for most of the close-range engagements. The US military used Israeli-developed tactics and the lessons of 1973 to refine battlesight shooting as the primary means of destroying enemy tanks, rather than long-range duels. Effective battlefield tank gunnery includes having the right round in the breech, the M32 battlesight set for an appropriate range, putting the crosshairs on the bottom-center of the target, and then firing without ranging. The commander uses the single commander's control handle to rotate the turret (handle left or right) and elevate or depress the main gun (handle back or forward). He gives the order "Gunner! Battlesight! Tank!" If a round is not already loaded in the breech, he will specify the type of ammunition to be used. When the gunner hears the order, his first step is to set the fire-control computer to the correct type of ammunition. The loader ensures the safety switch is on, then pulls back the breech operating handle until the breechblock is latched open. He checks the chamber is empty and clean. For ranges of 1,200m or less, the gunner will look through the M32 battlesight periscope, selecting the correct reticle, one for APDS and HEP, and one for HEAT. This method was used for almost all engagements in 1973 and all in 1991. The gunner puts the correct aiming crosshairs on the center mass of the target. If the gunner needs to use the M17A1 stereo coincidence rangefinder, he puts his eye to the rangefinder eyepiece – his forehead against the black cushioning – and when he sees the target the commander has ordered engaged he announces "identified." He rotates the range knob until the two images

he sees of the target – one solid and one "ghost" – combine into one clear image. (The commander also has a stereo coincidence rangefinder in his cupola and a control enabling him to traverse and fire the main gun.)

When the gunner announces "identified," the loader removes a heavy unitary 105mm round – like a huge rifle bullet – from the floor ready rack or from the turret bustle, reaching through the small blast door that separates the ammunition stowed there from the crew in the turret. With one hand at the back of the projectile and the other at the rear of the propellant case (originally of brass, replaced in the late 1970s by an aluminum alloy), he carefully places the round in the chamber guide and then pushes it home into the breech, quickly removing his fingers from the automatically closing breechblock. He then switches off the safety and announces "Up!" and the type of round that is in the chamber.

The commander gives the order "Fire," or will use his own controls to fire the main gun. The gunner, having set the main gun switch to "on", pulls the finger triggers on the H-shaped gunner's control handles or the trigger on the manual elevation control handle. He will announce "On the way" to alert the commander to be looking at the target to see if it is hit. Often two rounds are fired in quick succession at any target. At ranges of 1,200m or less, however, the first round should be a target hit. Impact is announced by the bright flash of a kinetic energy hit or a chemical energy explosion. If not the gunner will use burst-on-target methods to observe where the projectile landed and apply corrections – if he does not see it, he announces "Lost," or, if the commander has observed the impact, the commander will give corrections, such as "Drop 200" or "Add 200."

remaining Iraqi armor regrouped and launched another attack. In the clearing visibility, this attack was hit by TOWs at longer range and disintegrated.

By 1100hrs, there was little left of the Iraqi 22nd Brigade: 50 tanks (mainly T-62s) and 22 APCs were lost, and 300 prisoners taken, without any Marine casualties. Other Marine units effectively destroyed the remainder of the 5th Mechanized Division, mainly equipped with T-55 and Chinese Type 59 tanks. Major John Turner, TF Papa Bear's operations officer, recorded: "During the battle we encountered only T-55 tanks and Type 63/63C armored personnel carriers … of which I saw many. While the tanks were dirty, the ammunition inside appeared to be newly issued as the casings were clean and bright… The Iraqi tank gunners were poor shots. The Marine tank and TOW gunners never gave them a chance for a second shot." Marine Captain Dennis Green said, "The Iraqis were real poor gunners. Their tank gunnery skills just stunk.… They just don't hit people." The Marines also found that kinetic energy rounds could penetrate any Iraqi tank. They typically passed through the vehicle, causing damage that resulted in a catastrophic explosion one to four minutes later. HEAT or HEP rounds usually yielded instant destruction.

After the counterattack at the Al Burqan oil fields, the 1st Marine Division resumed its advance northwards into Kuwait. TFs Ripper and Papa Bear both encountered and hit numerous Iraqi tanks, many dug-in, including those that had been previously knocked out by the air campaign or had been abandoned by their crews. The Iraqi 3rd Armored Division now received new orders – it was to be the rearguard to Iraqi forces' withdrawal from Kuwait to Basra.

On the second day of the US advance, the M60A1s encountered and destroyed more Iraqi tank units. One of the tanks that shot it out with the Marines was the T-62 command tank of a T-55 tank unit knocked out by the 3rd Tank Battalion, which, as it advanced toward Kuwait International Airport, encountered increasing resistance as well as more crowds of surrendering Iraqis. The M60A1 of 1st Lieutenant Charles Freitus, Company C, 3rd Tank Battalion, took a near miss from an artillery shell: "Our sponson box and the right rear fender were badly mangled, shrapnel holed and littered the gear stowed aft of the turret in the basket and some of the antenna cables were sliced apart."

On the Marines' left flank, in the afternoon, the 2nd Marine Division's M60A1s pushed forward, defeating Iraqi tanks in a battle near a defensive position known as

M60A1 RISE Passive tanks of the 1st Tank Battalion lead the 1st Marine Division as it approaches its objectives on February 26, the third day of the ground war. While these tanks are moving cross-country, they are following in the tracks of the tanks in front of them to avoid mines. (US DoD photo by LCpl R. Price)

the Ice Tray. One M60A1 platoon from the 8th Battalion knocked out 13 Iraqi tanks. Yet as they advanced away from the oil fires, a combination of smoke, dust, and haze limited visual and infrared range to less than 1,000m. The M60A1's M17A1 stereo coincidence optical rangefinder was unable to function normally – like a rangefinder camera, it required moving a range dial until a "ghost" image was superimposed on the actual one – and engagements had to be carried out with the M32 battlesight, which proved to be effective.

The 1st Marine Division's tanks reached Kuwait International Airport in the afternoon and moved to cut if off before occupying it. They encountered what was left of the Iraqi 3rd Armored Division. Defending the airport was the 12th Armored Brigade with its T-72s – it quickly lost the 30–40 that were still operational. T-62s were encountered in dispersed and understrength platoon and company units. Most of those operational were knocked out by TOWs at long range. Other M60A1s were called on to breach the airport's defenses with mine rollers and MCLCs. The 1st Tank Battalion fought its way into the airport, though the area was not consolidated until after daylight on the third day of the conflict.

By the end of the day, the 3rd Armored Division had effectively ceased to exist; its losses included more than 250 T-55/62s and 70 T-72s. By the next day, the Iraqi withdrawal of the division was to cover became a rout, on what became known as the "Highway of Death" back to Iraq.

On the third day, as the 1st Marine Division held positions in and around Kuwait International Airport, the 2nd Marine Division had liberated the city of Al Jahra then pushed on to occupy the high ground on the Mutla Ridge to the northwest of the city, cutting off the Iraqi escape route from Kuwait to Basra. Most of the 166 Iraqi tanks claimed that day by the division were knocked out by M1A1 tanks.

The third day was the last day of combat for the Marines and their M60A1s. The 1st Tank Battalion's M60A1s claimed 50 Iraqi T-55 and T-62 tanks and 25 APCs. The 3rd claimed 57 T-55s and T-62s (plus five T-72s), seven APCs, and ten trucks destroyed, mostly at ranges of under 1,000m. The 8th destroyed more than three dozen tanks and a number of other vehicles. The longest-range engagements, by the 3rd, were at 1,400m, although an M60A3 in the 1st destroyed a vehicle at 3,200m range. Because the M60A1 lacked the M1A1's advanced thermal vision system, all its engagements were fought under daylight conditions. No Marine M60A1 or any other

Three knocked-out Iraqi Army T-62s silhouetted by the setting sun. (US DoD)

This Iraqi Army T-62 – possibly without unit markings (it has a camouflage net wrapped around its gun barrel) – was part of the massive unsuccessful Iraqi retreat from Kuwait on the third day of the ground war, that ended up on the "Highway of Death" past Mutla Ridge to Iraq. As with most vehicles, it was apparently abandoned when airstrikes blocked the road. (US DoD)

Marine armored fighting vehicle was hit by an Iraqi tank or antitank weapon. No Blazer boxes were detonated by enemy action. A total of ten M60A1s (five of which had been mounting mine clearance equipment) were lost, all to mines. Four were able to be repaired.

Also taking part in the liberation of Kuwait were Egyptian and Saudi M60A3s. These advanced into Kuwait to the west and east of the two Marine divisions, respectively, in a slow and methodical advance that encountered a few Iraqi tanks. They were able to enter Kuwait City, when the conflict ended.

M60A1 IN T-62 SIGHTS

Iraqi General Ra'ad Hamdani commented on the armored engagement: "We had the problem of inflexibility of usage with the armored forces; we always favored tying the infantry to tank divisions. This is the nature of the third world generals; they are not creative when it comes to maneuvering." Enough Iraqi T-62s survived 1991 to constitute a significant part of the armored force defeated by coalition forces in 2003's Operation *Iraqi Freedom*. The Marines re-equipped with M1 series tanks soon after 1991. The last M60A3s left service with National Guard armored units in 1997 and training units in 2004.

This artwork shows what one of the lead tanks of the Egyptian 25th Armored Brigade might have seen in the opening stages of the October 17 battle during the 1973 war. The T-62's TSh2B-41u telescopic sight is the gunner's primary sight. Here we see how it would appear to a gunner about to engage an M60A1 at 1,600m range, after the gunner has received the command from the tank commander as to the target, its range, and the type of ammunition to use. The tank commander would search for targets with his TKN-3 sight and the gunner would use his rotating MK-4 periscope to search from the other side of the tank. The driver and loader would look to the front through their periscopes. Anyone spotting a target announces its identification and bearing over the intercom. The commander and the gunner can then traverse the turret. If the tank commander is rotating the turret, he announces "Override, left (or right)" over the intercom and depresses the override button on the TKN-3's left handgrip. He can traverse the gun, but cannot fire or elevate it. When the target enters the sight picture of the gunner's TSh2B-41u sight, he announces "Identified" over the intercom.

The tank commander will normally determine the range if this is required, using the rangefinding stadia of the TKN-3, if the target is approximately 2.7m high (the height of an M60). He brackets the target's top with the appropriate stadia line, each labeled in hundred of meters range. If the target's height is substantially different from 2.7m – such as a hull-down tank – he must use the 4-mil azimuth scale and a formula to determine range. The gunner's sight has a similar rangefinding stadia and he can determine the range if required.

After the commander has determined the range, he gives the fire command, including target, ammunition, range, and direction. The gunner then elevates the gun, so that the horizontal range line on the sight reflects the range to the target. Against tank targets, it is normally kept at the 1,600m line because of the flat trajectory of the BR-5 APFSDS projectile. If the gun is not yet loaded, the loader will now half turn or use his left hand – the loader is to the right of the gun – and take a round from the ready ammunition racks clipped to the turret sides. He guides the large round halfway into the breech with both hands and then seats it with a vigorous shove, snatching his hand back from the rapidly closing horizontal breechblock. Throughout the loading process, the gun is automatically elevated to 2–5 degrees' elevation to provide access to the breech. The gun cannot use power traverse until the loader has chambered the round and depressed the safety to "fire." The gunner can then track a moving target using his power control or use the sight's lead lines to lead a moving target. He next selects the main gun switch, which turns on the automatic shell extraction, and announces over the intercom "Ready."

The tank commander orders "Fire." The gunner presses the electrical trigger on the right handgrip of his controls or, alternatively, the manual triggers on the elevation handcrank or on the gun itself. The gun fires and, upon recoil, the breech opens and ejects the spent shell brass casing into the automatic ejection tray, where it is seized by grippers. The ejection tray elevates and the ejection port hatch in the rear of the turret opens. The ejector propels the casing at great speed through the open port, which then closes. If it is out of alignment, due to rapid movement over rough terrain, the casing will miss the port and instead hit the turret wall, rebounding in the direction of the loader or gunner.

CONCLUSION

The battles between M60s and T-62s were shaped by the reality of the Cold War. The US and Soviet militaries that developed the tanks were not primarily the ones to use them in battle. Yet the nature of superpower competition meant that learning from the results of tank battles in proxy or peripheral conflicts was vital to assuring the continued viability of their own forces.

Development of opposing systems can be as much a duel as anything on the battlefield. In the 1973 war, the Arab and Israeli armies used tanks the superpowers had developed for their own forces to use in a possible European conflict. The fit

M60A3 TTSs remain in service with the Egyptian Army and many other allied and friendly forces. In *Bright Star 01–02* in 2002, this Spanish Marines M60A3 TTS tank demonstrated beach-crossing skills while exercising in Egypt. (US DoD)

between the European model and the realities of tank duels in the Sinai proved problematic. As a result, the Israelis invested heavily to ensure that they no longer had to rely on this "duel" of tank development being fought by others for them. They would develop their own tanks. They did this with the post-1973 Magach upgrades of the M60 series and the indigenous Merkava design. The Egyptians, with a less-developed industrial base, have continued to rely on tanks designed by others. Egypt has increasingly participated in building or upgrading the tanks used by its forces.

Both the M60 and T-62 were developed as interim solutions, designed to counter new threats challenging the older M48 and T-54/55 tanks, which made up the bulk of the Cold War armored inventory. The intention was to replace both with more complex tanks, including those armed with ATGMs. In reality, both ended up as critical parts of the theater balance for decades. While the iterative aspects of development were important, decisions made at the outset shaped how they were used in combat. The Marines in 1991, for example, greatly regretted the M60A1's lack of an NBC protection system and the need to improvise engineer equipment, both the result of the tank being considered an interim design back in the 1950s.

Abandoned Iraqi T-62 in 1991, from the 2nd Regiment, 30th Armored Brigade, 6th Armored Division. It displays Chinese-designed sawtooth armored side skirts that were mounted by some Iraqi T-62s. (Roddy de Normann via Stephen Sewell)

In the postwar era, tanks became increasingly lethal when compared to their world war predecessors. The US Army calculated that a 76mm-armed World War II-era tank would have had to fire 13 rounds to obtain a 50 percent probability of a hit on a standing tank at 1,500m range; the 90mm-armed tanks of the 1950s required three rounds to achieve the same results, and the M60, only a single 105mm round. The results of the duel of tank development made the duels on the battlefield quick and deadly.

The duel between M60s and T-62s in Germany's Fulda Gap never took place. The Soviets had better resources and training than any of the countries that used the T-62 in sustained combat, although their forces had their own limitations, as fighting in Afghanistan demonstrated. But the threat posed by the T-62 as part of the build-up in Soviet theater war-fighting capability transformed the US post-Vietnam "hollow forces" into the well-trained and equipped ones of the concluding years of the Cold War. The US "won" the duel of developing tanks and enabling their use.

The results of the two kinetic tank duels were both tremendously one-sided. Both at the Chinese Farm and in the liberation of Kuwait, Israeli and US M60A1s wiped out large numbers of T-62s with minimal loss, with only a single possible M60 loss to a T-62. These outcomes reflected less the comparable strengths and limitations of the two tank designs and more the nature of the opposing forces. The Israelis and Americans were, at the tactical and operational levels, much better prepared, trained, and competent compared to their opponents. The tactics, techniques, and procedures of Israeli and US tankers repeatedly prevented the capabilities inherent in the T-62 design from having any effect in the form of knocked-out tanks. While the T-62 design was, on paper, just as capable as the M60A1, better gunnery and more effective tactics provided lopsided results. In the words of Brigadier General Crow, "at the end of the day, the best trained and drilled crews would carry the day."

BIBLIOGRAPHY

Abouseada, Handy Sobhy, *The Crossing of the Suez Canal, October 6, 1973*,
   Masters thesis, US Army War College (April 2000)
Adan, Avraham, *The Banks of the Suez*, Novato CA, Presidio (1984)
Bar-Joseph, Uri, "Strategic Surprise or Fundamental Flaws? The Source of Israel's
   Military Defeat at the Beginning of the 1973 War," *Journal of Military History*
   (April 2007)
Bronfield, Saul, "Fighting Outnumbered: the Impact of the Yom Kippur War on
   the US Army," *Journal of Military History* (April 2007)
Cameron, Robert S., "Pushing the Envelope of Battlefield Superiority – American
   Tank Development from the 1970s to the Present," *Armor* (November–
   December 1999)
Cureton, Charles, *With the 1st Marine Division in Desert Shield and Desert Storm*,
   Washington DC, GPO (1992)
Department of the Army, *Operator's Manual, Tank, Combat, Full-Tracked, 105mm
   Gun, M60*, TM-9-2350-260-10-1/2/3 (3 vols), Washington DC (February 1981)
Dinackus, Thomas D., *Order of Battle – Allied Ground Forces of Operation Desert
   Storm*, Central Point, OR, Hellgate (2000)
Dupuy, Trevor, *Elusive Victory*, New York, Harper & Row (1978)
e-Rewany, Hassan Ahamed, *The Ramadan War – End of an Illusion*, Masters thesis,
   US Army War College (2001)
Estes, Kenneth W., *Marines under Armor*, Annapolis, MD, Naval Institute Press (2000)
Frietus, Joe, *Dial 911 Marines: Adventures of a Tank Company in Desert Shield and
   Desert Storm*, McCarran, NV, New American Publishing (2002)
Garwych, George W., *The 1973 Arab–Israeli War: The Albatross of Decisive Victory*,
   Leavenworth, KS, Combat Studies Institute Press (1996)

Herzog, Chaim, *The Arab–Israeli Wars*, London, Arms & Armour (1982)

Hunnicutt, R.P., *Abrams*, Novato, CA, Presidio (1990)

Hunnicutt, R.P. *Patton*, Novato, CA, Presidio (1984)

Isby, David C., *Weapons and Tactics of the Soviet Army*, London, Jane's (1988)

Isby, David C. & Charles Kamps, *Armies of NATO's Central Front*, London, Jane's (1986)

Lathrop, Richard & John McDonald, *M60 Main Battle Tank*, Oxford, Osprey (2003)

McGrath, John J. (ed.), *An Army at War: Change in the Midst of Conflict*, Leavenworth, KS, Combat Studies Institute Press (2005)

Mass, Michael, *Magach 6B Gal – M60A1 in IDF Service, Part 1*, n.p., Desert Eagle (2006)

Melson, Charles D., Evelyn A. Englander & David Dawson, *US Marines in the Persian Gulf 1990–91: Anthology and Annotated Bibliography*, Washington DC, GPO (1992)

Ministry of Defense USSR, *Tank T-62*, Moscow, Military Publishing (1978)

Moore, Molly, *A Woman at War*, New York, Scribner's (1993)

Mrocakowski, Dennis P., *With the 2nd Marine Division in Desert Shield and Desert Storm*, Washington DC, GPO (1993)

National Training Center, S-2 177th Armored Brigade, *The Iraqi Army: Organization and Tactics,* Fort Irwin, CA, 3 January 1991

O'Ballance, Edgar, *No Victor, No Vanquished*, San Rafael, CA, Presidio (1978)

Pollack, Kenneth M., *Arabs at War: Military Effectiveness 1948–1991*, Lincoln, NE, University of Nebraska (2002)

Post War Brief for Secretary of Defense – USMC Armored Vehicles, Washington DC (1991)

Rabinovich, Abraham, *The Yom Kippur War – The Epic Encounter That Transformed the Middle East*, New York, Schoken (2004)

Shazly, Saad el, *The Crossing of the Suez,* San Francisco, CA, American Mideast Research (1980)

Salter, Charles B. & Harry Spiro, *Evaluation of Silicious Cored Armor for the XM60 Tank*, Technical paper 11733, US Army, USATAC (8 November 1958, declassified 20 June 1979)

Smith, Matthew L., *Lessons Learned from 20th Century Tank Warfare: Does A Common Thread Exist?*, Masters thesis, US Army Command and Staff College, Fort Leavenworth, KS (1988)

Starry, Don & George F. Hofman (eds.), *Camp Colt to Desert Storm – The History of US Armored Forces*, Lawrence, KS, University of Kansas Press (1999)

US Army, *Battlefield Gunnery Techniques for Tanks*, Training Circular TC 17-13-3 (June 30, 1975)

US Army Command and Staff College, *Selected Reading in Tactics – The 1973 Middle East War*, Reference Book 100-2 (August 1976)

Ustyankov, Sergey V. & Dmitriy G. Kolmakov, *Tanki-60 kh* [Tanks of the 1960s], Nizhniy Tagil, Media-Print (2007)

Woods, Kevin M., Williamson Murray & Thomas Holday, *Project 1946*, Report D-3530, Alexandria, VA, Institute for Defense Analysis (December 2007)

Zaloga, Steven, *T-62 Main Battle Tank 1965–2005*, Oxford, Osprey (2009)

INDEX